BUSINESS
WELLBEING COACH

BUSINESS
WELLBEING COACH

Unity of Hexagons

Firdevs Dede

www.threedimensiondyslexia.org.uk
www.firdevsdede-dyslexia.com

Copyright © 2018 by Firdevs Dede
Front cover image (Digital Drawing) © Firdevs Dede 2017
Back cover photo © Firdevs Dede 2016
Table 1 (Emotional Intelligence Checklist) © Firdevs Dede 2016
Table 2 (MARA in Politics, 2018) © Firdevs Dede 2016
Table 3 (MARA in Education, 2018) © Firdevs Dede 2016
Spiritual Exercises (27 Stages) © Firdevs Dede 2016
The author has asserted her moral right under the Copyright, Designs and Patents Act, 1988, to be identified as the author of this work.

Correspondence address with the author
threedimensiondyslexia@outlook.com

Author's websites
www.threedimensiondyslexia.org.uk
www.firdevsdede-dyslexia.com
www.firdevsdede.com

Library of Congress Control Number:		2018906219	
ISBN:	Hardcover	978-1-9845-3038-7	
	Softcover	978-1-9845-3039-4	
	eBook	978-1-9845-3040-0	

All rights reserved. No part of this book may be reproduced or transmitted in any form or by any means, electronic or mechanical, including photocopying, recording, or by any information storage and retrieval system, without permission in writing from the copyright owner.

Scripture quotations marked NKJV are taken from the New King James Version. Copyright © 1982 by Thomas Nelson, Inc. Used by permission. All rights reserved.

Print information available on the last page.

1st edition published in Jun 2018

To order additional copies of this book, contact:
Xlibris
Tel: 1-888-795-4274
www.Xlibris.com
Orders@Xlibris.com

Contents

1) Acknowledgements ix
2) BWC's Mission (2018) xi
3) Unity of Hexagons xiii
4) Author's Introduction xv
5) Herd instinct isn't for survival any longer! 1
6) Selflessness is essential for a better relationship 4
7) Awareness of our spiritual identity shapes meaningful interactions 7
8) Compassion is the essence of wellbeing 11
9) Hotel management and fall of standard 16
10) Importance of ordinariness in life - 17 Oct 2015 19
11) The difference between positive & negative experiences 21
12) Health hazard and how we cope with it 24
13) Trade people & ethical work practice 29
14) Politics & Emotional Intelligence 31
15) Table 1 Emotional Intelligence Checklist in Politics ... 34
16) Table 2 Mood, Attitude, Responsibility, Action (MARA, 2018) 35
17) How to stay objective in politics 36
18) History shouldn't repeat itself! 38
19) Code of ministerial practice in politics 43
20) Loss of political integrity & power of resilience 46
21) Corporate culture restricts disabled students' autonomy 50
22) Whose incompetence, disabled students or staff? ... 53
23) Table 3 Teaching Competence (MARA, 2018) 62

24) All genuine prayers are valid within cross-cultural context 63
25) Wellbeing investment plan is better than financial investment plan 68
26) Our life experiences are confined between time and space 72
27) Originality is misunderstood without any criteria for it ...75
28) Breaking glass ceilings doesn't mean breaking cultural inequalities...78
29) Academic curriculums and mental health......................83
30) Reflection on practical experience 86
31) We don't possess anything except our memories 92
32) Ransomware hackers corrupt their intelligence.............95
33) All types of extremism are harmful!................................98
34) Equality Act 2010 has been challenged! 105
35) What is your focal point today? 115
36) Robots with emotional intelligence! 120
37) Market Share..124
38) Are we getting there or not?...132
39) Whistleblowing at work...135
40) Special Days – 21 Feb 2018 146
41) Miraculous events do occur as well as cynical ones in life! 151
42) Numerical Values 155
43) Spiritual Awareness Exercise – Stage 1 161
What level of awareness are you experiencing in your spiritual identity?...161
44) Spiritual Awareness Exercise – Stage 2 163
Identifying the positive energy. 163
45) Spiritual Awareness Exercise – Stage 3 166
Listen to the peaceful silence of calmness.............166
46) Spiritual Awareness Exercise – Stage 4 169
The origin of spiritual existence................................169
47) Spiritual Awareness Exercise – Stage 5 171
How to increase your awareness of spiritual identities of others....171

48) Spiritual Awareness Exercise – Stage 6 174
    How strongly are you connected to spiritual power? 174
49) Spiritual Awareness Exercise – Stage 7 177
    How do you monitor your spiritual conscious? 177
50) Spiritual Awareness Exercise – Stage 8 180
    How satisfied are you with what you have got? 180
51) Spiritual Awareness Exercise – Stage 9 182
    Spiritual consciousness for food intake 182
52) Spiritual Awareness Exercise – Stage 10 184
    How thankful are you for the gifts you possess? 184
53) Spiritual Awareness Exercise – Stage 11 187
    The hypothetical questions 187
54) Spiritual Awareness Exercise – Stage 12 191
    Daily spiritual goals 191
55) Spiritual Awareness Exercise – Stage 13 194
    The dimension of spiritual goals for inclusiveness 194
56) Spiritual Awareness Exercise – Stage 14 196
    Readiness to share spiritual awareness with others 196
57) Spiritual Awareness Exercise – Stage 15 199
    Recording spiritual accomplishments 199
58) Spiritual Awareness Exercise – Stage 16 201
    Differentiation of spiritual awareness 201
59) Spiritual Awareness Exercise – Stage 17 203
    Finding inner peace through spiritual wisdom 203
60) Spiritual Awareness Exercise – Stage 18 205
    Connecting to our common ancestors via a spiritual tree 205
61) Spiritual Awareness Exercise – Stage 19 207
    Invisible connections through meditations 207
62) Spiritual Awareness Exercise – Stage 20 210
    Locate your spiritual connection with our common ancestors 210
63) Spiritual Awareness Exercise – Stage 21 212
    Identify the depth of your spiritual connections 212

64) Spiritual Awareness Exercise – Stage 22 214
    Spiritual joke and spiritual joy 214
65) Spiritual Awareness Exercise – Stage 23 215
    Uniqueness of your spiritual awareness 215
66) Spiritual Awareness Exercise – Stage 24 216
    Monitor your current state of spiritual mood 216
67) Spiritual Awareness Exercise – Stage 25 217
    Self-assessment of your spiritual growth 217
68) Spiritual Awareness Exercise – Stage 26 218
    Self-evaluation 218
69) Spiritual Awareness – Stage 27 221
    Unity of Hexagons 221
70) Press Review, 2011 223
71) Peer Review on Amazon, 2015 226
72) Peer Review on Xlibris, 2011 227
73) Press Review, 2015 228
74) Peer Review on Amazon, 2015 231
75) Press Review, 2012 235
76) Genre: Modern Poetry 237
77) Peer Review, 2012 238
78) Genre: Non-Fiction 239
79) Firdevs Dede's Services, 2018 241
80) Firdevs Dede's Profile 245
81) References 249
82) Forthcoming Publication, 2019 253

Acknowledgements

I would like to express my gratitude to all my MA and BA students who kindly provided me regular feedback of their needs; the problems they face during their academic studies and their aspirations for future developments. This book is based on my personal experience as part of my reflective diary of evidence-based research I had undertaken since 2015. I am solely responsible for the contents of the articles complied in this research study which is autobiographical. I was particularly careful not to offend any individual or organisations when I needed to highlight what worked well and what went wrong with a critical approach to practice. Academic integrity demands non-biased feedback in order to increase ethical practice and fairness. I hope that my criticism will be taken as a constructive feedback for the individuals and institutions to improve the standards of delivery in services from arts; literature; LMS size businesses/enterprises to education in the 21st Century.

I am truly grateful to my colleagues Dr. Sheren Abdulrahman and Dr. Maheshika Halbeisen for their encouragement to include their book reviews in this book entitled Business **Wellbeing Coach, Unity of Hexagons**. I appreciate Dr. Abdulrahman and Dr. Halbeisen's kindness and generosity for reading my publications and sharing their views with me and general public.

I declare that my publisher, Xlibris Corporation, is not responsible for the contents of my research book. I thank Xlibris Publication Team for enabling me to publish my practical research with the best intention of serving general public, academics and consumers of services & goods. I appreciate my publisher's commitment to my success.

Firdevs Dede, 2018

BWC's Mission (2018)

Business Wellbeing Coach (BWC) or Unity of Hexagons is a non-profit and non-political voluntary organization. BWC focuses on individuals' wellbeing through awareness of spiritual identity, educational development in arts, social science, Information Technology and meaningful, ethical business transactions as participants with inner peace. BWC encourages to overcome the barriers the disadvantaged members of the society experience with hidden disabilities such as dyslexia, anxiety disorder, cognitive aging, mental health problems, poverty, a lack of opportunities through innovation in business, arts, craft and social science. The expected outcome of participants is the growing satisfaction in cultural and scientific developments by expanding their spiritual IQs within democratic, multi-faith and multi-cultural environments of education & workplace in peacetime.

Objectives

To encourage internal peace and understanding of shared human history by relating to our common ancestors.

To deliver development programs in wellbeing strategies through specialist coaching.

To promote equal opportunities for the least fortunate members to participate in cultural exchange.

To create a value for the members through one-to-one interactions such as talking therapy, art therapy, drama therapy, photography, literature and poetry recitals.

To offer advocacy service to the members with hidden disabilities such as dyslexia, dyspraxia, dyscalculia, anxiety disorder, depression, manageable mental health conditions and cognitive aging for increasing awareness of their legal entitlements for an inclusive learning environment.

To engage with structured research programs in arts, social science, spiritual development, occupational therapy and work ethics.

To organize World Heritage Site Excursions for educational research purposes to increase awareness of world cultural heritage in peacetime.

To facilitate learning with sustainable survival budget in order to enjoy debt-free life.

Unity of Hexagons

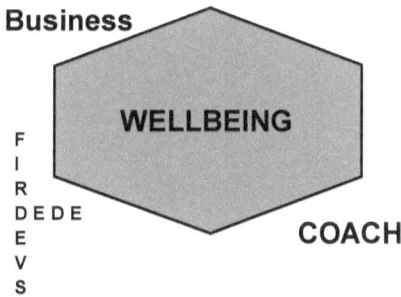

External PEACE is the reflection of our spiritual conscious within the universe.

I dedicated this book to the most peaceful and spiritually wealthy people who have contributed to the good causes relentlessly in line with God's purposes without getting side-tracked by any merciless destruction, violence or negative energy. Let's stay in touch with good spirits of all humankind in peace, divine joy, divine love, divine creativity and an unshakable confidence for a better future! God Bless peaceful people with the divine gift of UNCONDITIONAL LOVE for humanity and enduring animals of our time!

Firdevs Dede, Apr 2018

Author's Introduction

Business Wellbeing Coach or Unity of Hexagons is based on my firsthand experience of dynamic interactions with my colleagues; writers, poets, painters, composers, fashion designers, actors, architects, counselors, lecturers, trainers, doctors, nurses, therapists, librarians, retailers, coaches, legal professions, financial advisers, insurance officers, public speakers, immigrants, farmers, engineers, parents and my dear students from all over the world who have kept in touch with me during the last 37 years.

Human communication is a two-way process when we transmit and receive information at the same time. An ineffective communication process gets distracted by the social noise which has got the capacity of blurring our messages or ruining social interactions. Neither the receiver nor the transmitter benefits from a verbal interaction when the social noise is too destructive to consider our spiritual need to be understood. The social noise is experienced as prejudgment which misinterprets language clues including body language, unusual facial expressions, cultural barriers and an inadequate spiritual connection with one another while we are transmitting or receiving information. Unrealistic expectations of the transmitter and the receiver from a communication process can obscure the interaction by causing a low regard for one another's uniqueness due to a lack of spiritual experience with spiritual identities.

In the absence of a spiritual connection with a transmitter of data, it is impossible for a transmitter to get across their messages clearly to the responders within any industry from education to legal profession. Business Wellbeing Coach (BWC) focuses on how we read each other's messages through a spiritual connection. BWC increases productivity and eliminates a waste of human energy and financial resources. In this self-help resource book, I identify the difference between the effective communication skills and the breakdown of a meaningful communication process. Elimination of a two-way misunderstanding is possible through increasing our responsibilities when we specifically focus on spiritual awareness of the communication process. BWC or Unity of Hexagon is an essential read which will benefit anyone who consciously requires to master spiritual communication skills in order to improve social skills and increase competency at work. Unity of Hexagon is not intended to criticize formal religious practices as it is not a politicized spiritual book in the sense that the olden and modern spiritualist movements might have claimed. I do not make any assumptions about religious doctrines, ideology and practices. The contents of this book are based on my personal experience with the people who practice diverse religious beliefs in their own ways. I share my observations of the most common communication problems which were experienced at spiritual levels due to spiritual blockages of data transmitters during verbal interactions in peacetime outside the war zones.

Our daily realities could be more meaningful when we acknowledge ourselves with the combination of mind, body and spirit. During any business relationship from education to employment; from arts to social science and daily politics, participants usually are conditioned to ignore a spiritual connection with one another as a reaction to the politicized religious conflicts taking place all over the world. All forms of wars; World War I; World War II; Cold War I; Cold War II; Middle Eastern Cold War and civil wars are the manifestation of the communication breakdown with the extreme violation of civil rights. Unfortunately, formalized or politicized religious practices divided the whole humanity rather than keeping us together. Young generations are confused by the hatred promoted under the name of God when civil wars keep on breaking out because of different interpretations of religious practices. The human history has been established by the distractive outcomes of the religious divisions towards minority groups in the form of ethnic cleansing through genocide or mass murder. A genuine spiritual connection with one another has been made almost impossible because of the disconnection to our spiritual IDs which could be nourished by our special effort outside the falsity of religious hatred.

Removing a genuine spiritual ingredient from our daily communication process has been causing disastrous effects from mishandling the code of practice at work to abusing political power which usually turns the external realities into tragic human conditions such as the most recent civil war like the Syrian War with the international political conflict lingering over its eight-year duration. The statistical bad record of the Syrian War is 400,000 loss of human lives including children since the civil war has been started on 15th March 2011 (BBC, 2018). When some of us are turned into social fatalities struggling to find plausible answers for their sufferings within the unfair justice systems of the corrupted political games, we witness a lack of genuine compassion for the sufferers of the total communication breakdown which excludes a peaceful spiritual connection with one another.

Business Wellbeing Coach highlights what goes wrong with daily business interactions and how the meaningless violence could be reversed when our spiritual identity activates inner peace and makes us feel more than body and mind. I have included 27 exercises for readers to assess spiritual awareness of their unique spiritual IDs with self-evaluation about who we are and what we are capable of achieving through successful business relationships at a spiritually fulfilling level. Building up a brand-new communication system in each professional channel will eliminate the risk factors which usually threaten our civil liberties. Choosing to believe in omnipresence or supreme being of God is as abstract as non-figurative art. To be in line with Divine Power is more than a religious act but it is a healing art form. Once a believer finds a way to connect to their Creator through their developing spiritual IQs during daily meditation, their bodies and minds are healed beyond any medical attributes the medical profession invented for curing diseases of physical or mental dysfunctions. The power of our spiritual IDs will enhance our communication as alternative means to the unpleasant manipulative human power of language games with ineffective politics of noisy disruption.

An open-minded approach to spiritual awareness exercises will maximize the benefit of the suggested communication experience to achieve effective outcomes by leashing politicized religious biases. I wish you a satisfactory experience of an active engagement with our world and the most complex species of our fellow human beings like us and completely different from us through a rewarding spiritual connection! Let's hope human communication will be turned into an art form but not a shameful political destruction any longer! Recognizing the difference between a genuine communicator and a violent disrupter is the way forward. Thus, the human language could be utilized with spiritual awakening exercises to appeal readers' spirit by going beyond the mind and body experience.

Herd instinct isn't for survival any longer!

Human beings are social and spiritual individuals when they are able to place themselves within mature spiritual relationship at personal, communal, professional, national and international levels. Each level of spiritual maturity demands unity from group members to feel a sense of belonging which defines their own territory by the majority. Subsequently, it becomes almost impossible for individuals to act outside normative behaviors of their group which they conform within the boundary of their belief system as the extension of their group identity. The group identity usually develops through the kinship of a particular class, race, ethnicity, religion and educational, professional or employment backgrounds, with the same or similar socio-economic, spiritual, occupational and political common grounds. Developing a group identity has got positive and negative effects on individuals' spiritual maturity. Positive effect could be experienced as social inclusion among the same group members; negative effect could be experienced as social exclusion outside one's own ethnical or professional group. Group identity could also cause group biases towards other groups within the same community. When individuals stop monitoring their group biases, they face the danger of losing their autonomy for making non-biased decisions. Group behaviors attached to group biases could damage individuals' professional credibility in any occupation with human concerns such as politics, health and social care, legal system, education, training, housing, mentoring and business coaching. The herd instinct might jeopardize individuals' rights to be treated fairly without being perceived as a threat to the non-group members during any social and business interaction within a diverse community structure.

Our human subconscious is conditioned by the nature of our upbringing within the territorial spiritual background, which is limited to the group members' normative behavior. Once the individuals place themselves outside their own territorial boundary, they are obliged to monitor their limitations such as prejudgments which may be subconsciously accumulated by belonging to specific groups within the boundaries of spiritual or non-spiritual professional bodies. Professions like academics, legal practitioners, health specialists, religious leaders and politicians are unable to recognize their preconceptions of others with different normative behaviors. Consequently, they either under estimate or completely ignore other professions' contributions to spiritual development of the world community. Unfortunately, the herd instinct promotes a pragmatic outcome; it is easy to observe this negativity even within a philanthropic act of generosity which favors certain groups and excludes others who do not fit into the mainstream culture or subcultures.

A Business Wellbeing Coach facilitates self-monitoring of spiritual interactions with colleagues, supervisors, mentors, fellow coaches, trainers, trainees, employers, employees, service providers, service users, teachers, students, health professions, patients and clients consciously by encouraging everyone to identify their group biases which may be triggered by the herd instinct. When our spiritual biases are identified internally, it is necessary for us to take positive actions to remove group-disturbance as well as spiritual barriers preventing us from fulfilling our professional duties without being interfered by the herd instinct itself.

Selflessness is essential for a better relationship

Selflessness is the highest development of spiritual identity which could only be flourished beyond the normative expectations of the herd instinct within the group behavior of professions. A Business Wellbeing Coach needs to be fully aware of the power of the selfless commitment to clients' wellbeing rather than their own. No matter how hard it is to reduce the professional selfish desire of wanting to be acknowledged as a significant part of the coaching process, a Business Wellbeing Coach always acts as a selfless profession with less emphasis on self-importance without diluting their core professional values for serving others in the best capacity of their knowledge and experience that will ultimately bring the most successful coaching interactions. The selfless act of a Business Wellbeing Coach facilitates meaningful relationships with their clients who are enabled to see themselves equal to their coaches without the boundaries of the herd instincts of their separate group identities which might have shaped by their politics, class, race, gender, ethnicity and socio-economical circumstances. The quality of coaching relationship eases purposeful outcomes of the empowering connectivity in a business wellbeing coaching practice.

Just to give a few examples about selflessness here, I think of a selfless brain surgeon, who saved his patient's life by breaching the medical rules when he licked a hair on his patient's brain to prevent any accidental damage of her senses with a medical instrument. The patient who was unconscious during the surgical operation has never discovered the selflessness of her surgeon after being fully recovered from unbearably painful headaches because of the hair stuck on her brain before the unconventional brain surgery took place.

Another example of selflessness could be included here as an example from the real-life situation I read in a newspaper some time ago. A taxi driver acted like a midwife when his customer gave birth in his car on the way to hospital for childbirth. The driver didn't have any experience of the unusual situation he found himself by coincidence. He had to make a quick decision to save the child and the mother which brought a happy delivery under the most unusual circumstances. The taxi driver didn't get a fee for the delivery but he gained self-satisfaction out of his spiritual capability which provided a remarkable story to tell his friends that must have paid the highest spiritual dividend for his job appraisal.

There is no material value for selfless act that an average employee might be conditioned to expect under the influences of pragmatic relationships. When we compare and contrast unconventional marketing strategies to conventional aggressive marketing strategies, it is easier for us to experience a spiritual connection with client/customer/service user as nobody feels cheated or deceived in the absence of sale aggression. Unconventional marketing strategies promote selfless and caring relationship with potential or existing service users by valuing their needs for a transparent business transaction that appears as an alternative and meaningful practice to modern aggressive forces of market economy. Whereas, aggressive selling techniques breed greed by ignoring consumers' needs to be valued with respect and care for their wellbeing.

In a holistic business relationship, service users are not isolated from their whole life stories when they are offered professional services as they are treated with a unique consumer dignity for their value systems, race, gender and their spiritual needs in the way how they want to be seen but not how they are artificially perceived by the judgmental professions with group biases. An ethical business transaction offers an unconditional acceptance of each individual consumer with their uniqueness as they are not harassed by the forceful element of aggressive selling techniques. A successful business relationship builds up a trusting intervention between consumers and providers which increases wellbeing and positive energy without being deflated by the conventional demoralizing selling strategies.

Awareness of our spiritual identity shapes meaningful interactions

While I was thinking, breathing, practicing Business Wellbeing Coaching, I experienced a fraud scandal in 2015. I was devastated by the ruthlessness of the scam company owner. My website designer disappeared with my intellectual properties and bank details within less than 6 months of having my website online leaving me disappointed and angry. My sleeping pattern was disturbed by the unpleasant experience. My online business was ruined by the dishonest website designer overnight. I couldn't come to terms with the fact that unethical business people are capable of destroying their customers' dignity without any consideration for their clients' physical, mental, emotional, spiritual and financial wellbeing. The website company owner must have lacked a spiritual identity that was what I thought instantly. Without connecting to clients at a spiritual level, any business transaction could be ended with a fraud case which is described as wrongful or criminal deception intended to result in financial or personal gain in the New Oxford American Dictionary. I explored some more descriptions related to 'fraud' in order to handle the fraud case in writing as I needed to articulate what I experienced in a police report for preventing others from facing similar experiences.

Fraud Squad (n)
It is a division of a police force appointed to investigate fraud which I did not need to know until I faced the most convincing fraud case.

Fraudster (n)
A person who commits fraud, especially in business dealings.

Fraudulent (adj.)
Obtained, done by, or involving deception, especially criminal deception: fraudulent share dealing.

I wonder what motivates professional people to comply with code of ethics in any business domain without getting corrupted. Unlucky consumers who faced scam cases, often recorded how they felt after being ripped off. It was not the amount of the money they lost mattered to them but the amount of confidence they placed in corrupted individuals who cheated them. The unpleasant reality was too upsetting to accept somehow! Personally, I prefer not to engage in any deception rather than dealing with the aftermath of an abused verbal agreement which contradicts the unconditional trust factor of ethical practice. Is it possible for us to prevent ourselves from falling into traps of unethical business owners over and over again? Probably not! We live in a century of corruptions and scandalous fraud cases that weaken business relationships due to the unethical consumerism mania; materialistic expectation overshadows the spiritual innocence of unconditional trust some of us still place in complete strangers during business transactions. Consumers are treated as if they are unintelligent human beings with the lowest IQ which place them into a category of idiots that attracts common predators with criminal tendency to abuse any business relationship.

I wonder whose fault it was when I was cheated by numerous sham operations. Was it my fault or the fault of the corrupted pretentious business people who happened to be in my way and took advantage of my unconditional trust? How could we prevent the cycle of being tricked over and over again in our daily business transaction? I am afraid there isn't a written formula what to do and what not to do in any industry until we find ourselves trapped within extraordinary circumstances facing aggressive sellers' brutal tactics without any moral stance. Most of us are not streetwise enough to identify the unpredictable scam cases taking place in private and public sectors. The important fact is that dishonest people pretend honesty with a subtle craftiness. It is not easy to spot their tricks when they attempt to deceive us. While I was looking for concrete examples to demonstrate what I meant about dishonesty and aggressive selling techniques in this self-help book, I experienced the most unpleasant fraud cases one after another. Initially, I aimed to compile my firsthand experiences with unethical providers or suppliers within the most competitive and corrupted market places of the global industries. Then, I decided to focus on solutions rather than the problems. I disregarded some of my negative experiences with dishonest people in order to give a fair chance to potential business owners and consumers to treat one another with respect and courtesy without being conditioned by the negativity of unethical practices. I illustrated what Business Wellbeing Coaching requires with specific exercises to make it easier for readers to distinguish the difference between awareness of our spiritual identity and ignoring it which makes us susceptible to face the most unintelligent scam cases.

If any dishonest business person gains either money or fame out of fraudulent actions, the fortune will not stay with them forever as this has been proved by the statistical evidence which we all come across while reading the media coverages of scandal columns. The unethical traders are the ones who pay the most expensive price for their dishonesty when they fall out of grace eventually or when they go bust in their businesses with unrecoverable defeat of social stigma attached to their names. Is it worth taking all the risk of losing one's personal and professional integrity for short-term financial gains? I do not welcome any short-sighted big gains as I am fully aware of the fact that there is no light at the end of the tunnel once we take the wrong path. In any business relationships, partners rely on each other's goodwill which usually comes from a faithful acceptance of the Divine Justice but not necessarily the justice systems of imperfect human courts. If a dishonest person we are dealing with has a spiritual void which has been neglected by their circumstances, there is nothing that could connect them with their spiritual consciousness. Otherwise, they could have differentiated the difference between right and wrong before attempting to mislead anyone with their sham operations. The vital part of any business transaction depends on how well the level of spiritual commitment has been established for a mutual peace of mind experience. If there is no spiritual awareness in a coaching relationship, the coaching transaction could be turned into a humiliating experience of scam. A lack of spiritual connection to clients' need for a trusting relationship ends up with hurt, regret and vulgarity.

Compassion is the essence of wellbeing

When I was trying to come to terms with one fraud case, I experienced another fraud case within a short interval. The unethical service provider sold me his 2-day stock exchange training with the most expensive gold memory-stick which turned out to be not gold at all. It didn't occur to me that the USB wasn't made of gold while the trader claimed that it was a gold memory-stick in order to increase the value of his stock exchange training. When I got the memory-stick tested for its authenticity, I was told that it was fake which caused me distress and anger. I demanded a full refund for the training I enrolled by paying a large sum of money upfront under being pressurized with aggressive selling tactics at the premises of the aggressive training provider. Instead of receiving an apology for the unacceptable dishonesty, the unethical trader refused to pay me a full refund claiming that I signed the sale agreement in his premises. At the back of the sale agreement, it was written in small prints that any product or service sold in his premises cannot be refunded. I was not given a chance to read through the sale agreement and digest its implications in the likelihood of a scam case. The aggressive trader reassured us that we would not regret for enrolling on his short training. If we did not find the course contents useful he promised us a full refund. Everything looked like he was complying with consumers' statuary rights in the UK which should allow the consumers to change their minds within the cooling period that is a 2-week time after purchasing each product or service. However, it didn't take me a week to realize that by being pressurized to sign the sale agreement in his premises I was deceived to accept his fraudulence with a legal document. The unethical trader with aggressive selling tactics lost his credibility in my eye. I cannot trust a person who plays a trick on me by preparing a legal document to be signed by consumers in his premises and makes a healthy profit from an unhealthy business transaction. If the dishonest provider managed to get 10 people on his stock exchange training, he would have made a fortune without any legal obligation to give a full refund to his victims if they realized they were fooled like me and demanded for a full refund. Professor Katherine Hawley in her paper titled *Trust, Distrust, and Epistemic Injustice (2015)* explains how trust develops between any business transaction as follows:

> *"We trust people's words, and we trust their actions; to put things somewhat differently, we trust people as speakers (or as writers, as signers, etc.), and we trust people as actors."*
>
> Professor Katherine Hawley (2015), p.3

It always annoys me to find out how arrogant the offenders are in life! The most corrupted offenders assume that they cheat anyone without any responsibility to repair the damages caused to their victims. As long as their victims are not aware of their corruption, the corrupted criminals keep on repeating their fraudulent behavior until they are caught up and warned that how they are operating their business is not only illegal but also morally unethical. I was determined to exercise my consumer's statuary rights without giving up. I thought it would not cost me excessive time and money to recover from my losses. I was told by a consumer adviser that I signed a legal document and agreed his terms and conditions as what he sold me is unreturnable. I was shocked. If I did not have other commitments in my life to deal with at the time I was facing a fraud case I could have taken up the matter further and proved that he violated my consumer's rights by using aggressive selling tactics. One of his staff threatened me in writing if I take the matter further, they would sue me for libel. I had no time to waste with this fraudulent trader and his likeminded staff. I moved on; yet, he did not as I keep receiving the same training advertisements even long after unsubscribing his promotional packages. To lessen the pain of the unpleasant experience, I felt the need to write a poem about the fake gold memory-stick which could be turned into a valuable experience for me to reflect years later as a senior citizen. After all, everything counts at the end of our lifelong journey as all experiences regardless good or bad lead us somewhere where we could reassess each experience and remember what we faced at certain times of our human existence either with appreciation or regret.

In my Wellbeing and Business Coaching Practice, all my clients receive understanding of their current circumstances and empathy with compassion which is my top priority in order to free the clients from the feeling of being inadequate in the areas of their weaknesses. A Business Wellbeing Coach cannot afford to give wrong signals to their clients to make assumptions about themselves, their coach or their circumstances in which they found themselves accidentally. There is no error message imposed on clients with an unfilled expectation from a coaching interaction such as a fake gold memory-stick or getting rich quickly. A client learns to be true to themselves and accept their weaknesses as well as their strengths with clarity. Then, they are given a choice to work on their weaknesses. Nothing is disguised under different packages of unethical commercialism. My clients are free to make their decisions about what needs to be improved or what needs to be discarded during the emerging process of their true-self without losing their human dignity.

I remember how dutifully I committed myself to one of my valued clients while I was working with her for two academic years successfully. Because of her health conditions, she couldn't attend some of the sessions she booked in advance as she was unable to predict her circumstances. While she was feeling like a failure, I had no choice but approached her with compassion by risking my weekly earnings. I didn't take any client for the days she pre-booked me. When she cancelled her sessions, there was no penalty for that as I promised cheerfully. I did bear the consequences of the cancelled sessions over the two years period. Our sessions worked well with my commitment to her wellbeing. I was there when she needed me as long as she could make it. I delivered her support sessions on my annual leave in order to enable her to meet her deadlines as she was experiencing a lack of motivation, discipline and time management skills at the time. Her self-esteem increased gradually; she stretched her abilities and became one of my success stories with the tangible outcomes. I was very happy to hear that she achieved 1st class degree in psychology. When I reflect on my past memories, I don't have any regret for the unconditional commitment to my client's specific need despite the fact that I ended up losing several hundred pounds from my full earning capacity. Compassion is an essential ingredient of unconditional dedication to our clients' wellbeing within any spiritually fulfilling relationship. Earning a living out of our passion is one thing but earning our clients' trust is another which demands a therapeutic relationship with mutual respect for the transparent relationship that doesn't allow dishonesty or any type of social masking. In the academic paper titled *Therapeutic use of self: a model of the intentional relationship*, the authors Renee R. Taylor and Jane Melton (2009) suggest that the therapeutic relationship is a socially defined and personally interpreted interactive process between two individuals within publicly understood roles. Taylor & Melton outline the framework of a therapeutic relationship with the following responsibilities of a therapist.

- The appropriate definitions and boundaries of the therapeutic relationship are sustained, and
- Positive interpersonal relating such as trust, mutual respect and honesty characterize the relationship.

Renee R. Taylor & Jane Melton (2009), p.137

Business Wellbeing Coach creates a therapeutic relationship for clients to feel comfortable without worrying about the negative aspects of their unpredictable health conditions such as not being able to know whether or not they will be able to attend support sessions which are pre-booked. Business Wellbeing Coach works with sincere dedication to clients' wellbeing by committing to clients' welfare which might not be feasible for some other coaches who depend on regular income for their day-to-day survival within the unpredictable financial circumstances. That is why Business Wellbeing Coaching is not suitable for the people whose primary motivation is to make money in the expense of leaving out the benefits of spiritual fulfilment within a therapeutic relationship.

Hotel management and fall of standard

I discovered a beautiful country house hotel in Bournemouth overlooking the sea with a very well-kept garden in 2013. I enjoyed the pleasant homely atmosphere of the country house hotel with the stunning sea view. I thought it was more than a hotel for me with the lovely memories of a single clean room which had the essential furniture for me to enjoy. There was a personal touch quality in the small room. Even I do not wear make-up, I liked the idea of cotton make-up removers left in a tiny delicate box on the dressing table for female guests. Management team's professional attitude to pay attention to small details made me feel like staying in a home rather than a hotel. I remember spending the whole afternoon in the hotel garden reclining on a sun-lounger listening to the buzzing of honey bees with butterflies collecting pollen and nectar from flowers which brought me my precious childhood memories back from Turkish countryside. I loved the sound of field crickets and occasional dawn chorus. It felt like being placed in a paradise on earth surrounded with unspoiled wildlife.

In Jul 2017, I wanted to refresh my memories of Bournemouth and decided to stay in the same hotel. I was certain that nothing possibly would go wrong as my long-term memory was full of vivid memories from the country house hotel. Through several correspondences with the hotel manager, I booked a single room online. I thought I would have the same experience of customer satisfaction. I was wrong. The hotel manager welcomed me at the reception and he was too quick to take my suitcase while I was checking in at reception. Finding my suitcase placed on top of the bed was an upsetting experience. I was appalled by the insensitivity and unhygienic approach of the hotel manager. I instantly removed the suitcase from the bed to the floor which was dirty with stains and dust. I looked around the dusty room with revulsion. In the evening, I realized that the duvet was dirty and had a large hole on it. I was disillusioned. My holiday was ruined by the fallen standard of a single room with a 4-star price. I endured my stay in the unpleasant room for 2 nights without demanding a full refund. My past memories were faded away with the awful reality of what I was experiencing. Under ordinary circumstances, I would have demanded either a full refund or a better quality of room. Because of the manager's mature age, I didn't want to make a complaint against him or how he handled my suitcase as I didn't want to cause him offence. Nevertheless, I felt it was my duty to raise my concerns by filling up the customer's feedback form at the end of my stay, just in case, the hotel staff would reflect on it and improve the room quality for potential residents. I wish I had never returned the same hotel four years later with the assumption of finding the familiar high standard. It was a lack of work ethics what I experienced at the country house hotel in Bournemouth in 2017. If the domestic personnel made an effort to change the dirty and distressed duvet with the fresh and clean one, gave a good dust to the furniture as well as hoovering the carpet before my arrival, I wouldn't have felt cheated. I remember recommending the hotel to my friends in 2013. I am unwilling to recommend the same hotel with the fallen standard to anybody after what I experienced in 2017. The dirty room wasn't a good value for my hard-earned money. I hope the hotel management will hire a Business Wellbeing Coach for their staff to set a high standard for what is acceptable and what is not from a customer point of view. The hospitality industry will thrive if staff comply with work ethics which should include treating everyone with dignity and making sure everyone gets customer satisfaction regardless whether they stay in a single or double room for a short stay or longer. Spiritual maturity demands recognition of our customers' needs for a decent treatment with a good value as a return on their investment in our services or products.

Importance of ordinariness in life - 17 Oct 2015

I had many tasks I planned to do a day before yesterday; I aimed to finish them all at weekends. Instead, I decided to have a day off without worrying about anything. I deliberately woke up late. I cooked simple vegetable dishes and couscous with a plenty of fresh tomatoes and onions. I had my late breakfast with a sheer pleasure of having my homemade cooking with natural yoghurt. I started thinking about how much we neglect enjoying the ordinary routines of our daily life when simplicity is turned into unworthy commodity. It has been difficult for many of us to accept ordinary concepts in life under the extreme pressure of having a unique experience as part of exaggerated adverts about luxury. We are conditioned by the idea that we will be less happy if we enjoy an ordinary day without extra-ordinary event occurring in our lives. Eventless life has been overlooked somehow! We are accustomed to believe that it is tediously worthless to enjoy ordinariness without getting bored with it.

It feels good to be an ordinary person leading an ordinary life at least at weekends in order to keep up with work and life balance without stretching our breaking point. When we slow down intentionally but not forcefully, having a quality of time regularly increases our awareness of the most important fact which is how our body, mind and spirit combination has been affected by our hectic life style. If we allow ourselves to rest well at least once a week without risking our inner peace, our body starts renewing its vitality to cope with next week's race.

Time-conscious mind can't be totally idle. Forgetting the concept of time and our daily responsibilities completely for a short while needs to be learnt through consistent practice. Our generosity to our body, mind and spirit trio is as important as being selfless in Business Wellbeing Coaching Practice. We need to measure our own needs for a quality of time to enjoy a nourishing meal without feeling guilty about not being able to complete everything as we planned previously. There is another day and another weekend to prioritize the important tasks we aimed to finish last week. Thinking about mortality is the best indicator of the level of our tolerance for choosing less hectic life style at weekends. What would have happened if we have left one task incomplete last week? Nothing would have been more detrimental than not enjoying an ordinary meal at weekends with a peaceful enjoyment of spiritual contentment!

The difference between positive & negative experiences

I had a positive experience of being cared for early morning in my pedicurist hands in 2016. I have been seeing my pedicurist for more than 2 years for a regular treat. When she removed the hard skin from my soles attentively, I always felt satisfied with her gentle attitude to my foot care. I often worried about the final date for my regular treat which might come to the maturation in the case of leaving her profession or the possibility of my next move to another location. How fortunate I have been to find a pedicurist who has treated me with care which I didn't receive from other pedicurists I visited before. My pedicurist's commitment to my foot care makes me appreciate her unique qualities. I am fully aware of the fact that her service is valuable and cannot have a price tag with currency. Our verbal interaction is limited to a few sentences when her focus goes on my both feet eagerly to make me feel good. My pedicurist's professional attitude to take care of my feet in the best possible way made me connected to her in a spiritual way even I am not familiar with her spiritual belief system. Somehow, the essence of spiritual connection has been achieved by the blissful interaction with my pedicurist's considerate attitude towards my foot care. I felt that my pedicurist was a caring person and her service was genuinely comforting when I compared and contrasted her to the sloppy and careless pedicurists who didn't pay much attention neither to my feet nor how I felt about their thoughtless attitude towards my wellbeing.

I remember the disastrous experience with a footcare practitioner in 2013. After having a long day working as a specialist tutor and mentor visiting students in different locations and feeling the aching pain on my feet, I popped in a Chinese Reflexologist Clinique in London. A young Chinese receptionist asked me to pay upfront for half an hour reflexology treatment while a mature Chinese reflexologist accompanied me to the massage room and left me there on my own. A few minutes later, the inexperienced non-Chinese reflexologist who lacked a sense of duty or commitment to her client's need appeared. The young reflexologist told me her life story in details by using her hands in the air to describe what she meant with her insufficient English while I was in desperate need for a proper foot massage and wishing her hands used only for releasing the pain out of my feet in silence. I felt sorry for the inexperienced reflexologist's disappointment with her life circumstances; however, I couldn't help feeling sorry for myself for not being able to receive a proper reflexology treatment for my aching feet. I could easily take up the matter and make a complaint about how I felt for being treated by an inexperienced reflexologist who talked about her life story in the expense of neglecting her duty to take care of my foot. The receptionist was Chinese, the senior reflexologist was Chinese, the Clinique looked like Chinese, I was charged a full professional fee for the best reflexologist in London; yet, I was given the worst service I could possibly expect to receive from a young reflexologist. My moral value stopped me from taking an assertive action as I didn't want to hurt an inexperienced and insensitive reflexologist's fragile arrogance that cost me a great deal without getting the best value in return. It is unethical to treat someone with disrespect in a rather selfish way. I checked out the professional requirements of reflexology practitioners prepared by the British Reflexology Association (2017). The following points were neglected during my reflexology treatment.

Code of Conduct

Reflexology practitioners should at all times:

Respect the needs of the patient and work towards the benefit of the patient within the scope of reflexology without causing any detriment to the patient.

Code of Practice

All members are required to observe high standards of performance in their reflexology practice.

The British Reflexology Association (2017)

The balance is to know the difference between a positive experience and a negative one during any working relationship. The latter one always brings unsatisfactory results which could be eliminated with the help of wellbeing coaching strategies such as focusing on clients' needs for their priorities. If a client pays a lot of money for half an hour reflexology treatment, the priority of the client is to receive a professional foot care but not a talking therapy. The talkative reflexologist confused me by occupying my mind with a completely irrelevant topic which didn't match my expectation of seeing a reflexologist in the first place. I prefer total silence when my foot receives a decent foot care!

Health hazard and how we cope with it

I was determined to enjoy my weekend with the healing power of simply being happy and content with my life after having a nourishing home-made lunch. I left home to walk towards Greenland Pier. I sat down on a bench overlooking the river and read Ben Okri's book titled *Famish Road* for an hour. What a poverty Ben Okri depicted in his book! Poverty must be a universal tragedy for the sufferers to experience in the case of social marginalization, misfortunes, famine, gender inequality, unemployment and non-stop civil wars taking place all over the world in the 21st century. What makes some of us more able to cope with unacceptable life circumstances has something to do with spiritual maturity by accepting the fact that nothing lasts forever. Everything comes to its maturity regardless we experience fortune or misfortune. The power of visualization technique enables us to visualize our lives beyond materialistic limitations!

The pigeons came around to accompany me and didn't mind that I didn't bring bird seeds for them. I heard the beautiful sound of seagulls. Everything looked so simple and satisfactory at the same time. The wind made me shiver a bit. I had to interrupt my reading and walked down the river by the houseboats. I started filming the houseboats and recorded my comments on how I would have felt if I had lived on one of those houseboats on the river. I felt so good and I started singing with happiness as it was a happy day of mine. I came home with a fulfilment of being content and thanked my Creator for His blessings.

The most unfortunate thing happens in life when we experience the contrast between refined human virtues and vulgar destruction such as positive energy and negativity of violence at the same time. Consequently, our self-confidence can easily be diminished within one second. We need to monitor our mood and ask ourselves how to avoid external destruction such as environmental noise. Sometimes, not watching news on the TV is a simple answer for us to recharge our optimism and positive energy for another day. After having a pleasant day by the river, I decided to go to bed for a goodnight sleep to have a deep rest. I slept through the night without any worry for the next day.

Today is the beginning of a new springtime in 2016. Over my breakfast with vegetable, nuts, natural yoghurt and rice, I reflected on what makes me happy in life. I found the answer while I was pondering on my senses to enjoy what I am blessed with such as food, water, shelter for my daily survival but more importantly the most healing sound of the birds reaching me by surpassing the terrible noise of the vehicles and human beings. There were roadworkers who drilled the pavement in front of my flat on Friday with a demolition hammer or more colloquially-known as Kangos in British English. Roadworkers usually expose themselves to the pronounced vibration which causes the abnormalities of the blood-circulation in their fingers as named white fingers in the long-run. According to the unspecified medical evidence, roadworkers risk their respiratory health by breathing hazardous dust containing respirable crystalline silica which brings additional occupational health complications. According to the National Institute for Occupational Safety and Health (NIOSH, 2016) the unbearable smell of the asphalt emulsion that is a melting mixture of petroleum solvents with water, triggers the potential cancer-causing hazard. Unfortunately, knowing all the harmful effects of the asphalt emulsion on the human health does not stop some industries from the unsafe exposure to the harmful chemicals. It is necessary for health & safety staff to intervene with the harmful industries' negligence of their duties for providing the essential preventative measure to keep up with public health regulations. Otherwise, the roadworkers pay the high price of losing their health alongside the local residents who happen to live in the areas as the unhealthy construction work keeps on repeating itself for years without giving a healthy break for normality to bear the long-term environmental hazards. I remember seeing the young women with their babies breathing the awful smell of the asphalt emulsion as a result of the roadwork or the restoration of the old buildings in my local area. The residents with young children and the elderly population with low level of resistance to health hazards are affected the most. The local council avoids taking the necessary precaution measurement to save human lives and decrease the high bills for cancer treatments of the local residents being exposed to prolonged environmental pollution over the years.

When the human population and their environments are put in risk, I wonder how we expect to keep ourselves happy and satisfied with the hazardous politics. Is there any possibility for us to be content with the careless local authorities' destructiveness? I personally think that I am not satisfied with the local authorities' services to our local community. I believe our fundamental need for a clean and peaceful environment has been challenged on a daily basis. When we face the ruthless violation of our human dignity in the form of environmental hazards, we often find ourselves as the defenseless sufferers of the inconsiderate local authorities without any right to reject their harmful interventions with our respiratory health. I usually find a short-time solution for the environmental hazard I face by changing my immediate environment. I decided to take an escape route to Hyde Park that is linked to Royal Borough of Kensington and it hasn't got the same health hazard we are exposed to in South London. I needed to make a transitional shift from the environmentally hazardous local area to the environmentally-friendly area of Kensington with a pleasant wild life. During the time I spent in Hyde Park, I detoxified my body, mind and spirit from the local health hazard. I realized that I was coaching myself with the wellbeing coaching strategies in a park free from the destruction of modern urban life.

A public tragedy took place in London on 14 Jun 2017. The 24-storey Grenfell Tower with 120 flats accommodated the residents on low incomes was on fire. The dramatic images of the disappearing tower were heartbreaking. It was understood that the high-rise block was built in 1974, renovated in 2016. The cost of renovation was £8.7 million. However, the renovation plan didn't take into account a proper fire-safety prevention which could have prevented the tragic death of 71 residents. The unfortunate residents lost their lives in the most distressing and painful circumstances. According to the British media (BBC, 2017), authorities in different boroughs are prepared to spend £343 million to make social housing safer in London in the near future. The surviving residents are placed in temporary accommodations. Most of them are facing an uncertain future. They've learned that it is not possible to put their hope in uncaring politicians or business people whose priorities were different than the residents' safety and wellbeing. When people are trapped in helpless situations without any escape route to get out of the tragic circumstances, there is one thing left for them to comfort themselves with which is internal peace. Business Wellbeing Coach offers an alternative way of dealing with problems while being confronted with the trap-like situations in the dysfunctional aftermath of selfish modernity. Learning how to survive without losing our human dignity even in the most undignified situations is an essential surviving skill which could be achieved by experimenting with wellbeing strategies such as visualizing better living conditions and getting involved with changing our immediate environments through positive actions. Pressure groups could be formed by the local residents to submit their wish list to the authorities including what they really need and what should be avoided while facing each tragedy without being sidetracked by the cruelty of political hazards.

Trade people & ethical work practice

We all depend on trade people's skills, experiences and goodwill not only at work or on vacation but also within our domestic environment. I wonder who didn't look for a plumber, a carpet fitter, a home decorator or a computer engineer over the years to unplug the sink; replace the broken taps or the fallen tiles; fit a new carpet; paint the kitchen or fix electronic gadgets. I often think how badly these individuals are treated without being appreciated; in some cases, their inputs towards our wellbeing are usually taken for granted. There is no written guideline for us to check against the criteria on what ethical work practice means when we look for an experienced and honest trade person to provide their services regularly or occasionally. We hope that things go well assuming the trade person knows their trade well enough to resolve the maintenance problem of our domestic environment without causing us any offence or further complications.

I met many unethical trade people who failed to meet the criteria for ethical work practice. I felt I was mistreated because of unethical trade people's falling standards. Some of them didn't come on the date and at the time they promised to do the job or they left the incomplete job without fulfilling their promises. Once I hired a person to replace the fallen tiles in my bathroom. The unprofessional trade person took his time and didn't complete the job on time. He didn't come back to finish the work within the period I took my annual leave. I had to go back to work without my bathroom properly fixed.

I also met excellent trade people who were skillful and complied with work ethics by paying attention to core values of their trades including time management, keeping up with their promises and doing their best to resolve the problems without causing me any inconvenience or offence. Business Wellbeing Coach differentiates between ethical and unethical practices. More importantly, it brings a clear guideline to identify what needs to be considered before hiring a trade person in order to prevent the unpleasant experiences with suppliers or providers for carrying out building maintenance within our domestic realities. It is like having a Chartered Quantity Surveyor who makes sure everything will go smoothly whether it is a brand-new property or an old building which needs a major renovation.

Politics & Emotional Intelligence

If we examine the weaknesses of the incompetent politicians in the world history, it is easy to identify a common defect which is a lack of emotional intelligence as the majority of the world politicians neglected to nurture their emotional intelligence for centuries. Unfortunately, unsuccessful politicians don't experience an empathetic connection with the majority of the average voters who are unable to find any common ground with the superficial politicians.

Politicians' success doesn't depend on how smart they might sound in their intellectual reasoning about what causes poverty, economic disasters, nuclear war threats or environmental inconsistencies experienced locally and globally in the 21st century but also whether or not they possess sufficient emotional intelligence as part of their cognitive profile. Intellectual competence doesn't compensate the current shortage of emotional intelligence amongst inefficient politicians in the global political arena. Many of the unsuccessful politicians are unable to relate themselves to the average people who might have unparalleled backgrounds with different race, class, gender, status, disabilities and deprivations of all kinds.

Successful politicians should be able to recognize the fact that no matter how cleverly they present themselves to the general public as confident and capable of resolving the problems with speed and accuracy, the outcome of their actions always speak louder. If ordinary citizens don't see much improvement in their living conditions in terms of having an access to adequate accommodation, work, transport, education, treatment, pension and green environment for sustainable daily survival, they wouldn't be impressed by politicians' false promises given under the extreme pressure of the election time. In the 21st century, politicians need to take up additional responsibilities for finding workable, practical solutions to the question of how to generate adequate financial resources for everyone to live comfortably so that poverty wouldn't cause civil wars or WW3 in the near future or unknown period of time. Politicians' roles need to be less bureaucratic but more practical in terms of problem solving skills on a day-to-day basis. Otherwise, they are unable to convince the general public for their good intentions when they are elected.

It is a tragic situation for average citizens to realize that the political candidates assigned to powerful positions by promising to resolve the most detrimental problems of economy locally or globally if the politicians can't keep up with their promises when they are in power. The powerless citizens are the ones who bear the burden of the financial crisis, war threats and environmental disasters with their declining life standards due to the consequences of short-sighted policies without long-term plans for sustainable national and world resources. Potential leaders should experiment with emotional intelligence exercises before finding themselves on a political platform to deliver their unconvincing speeches to the skeptical general public who are disappointed with the impractical political resolutions offered by the former politicians without seeing any improvement in their living conditions.

If a politician cannot visualize themselves in the awkward place of an average citizen with low income, there will be a conflict of interest in terms of outcomes such as what an average voter from diverse backgrounds demands and an incompetent politician's inability to fulfil this demand. It is like offering an expensive toy to starving children who are facing their mortality due to the scarcity of food and contaminated water or offering an affordable house insurance to homeless citizens. Politicians could get away with their weaknesses such as absence of degree in politics, economics, diplomatic relationship, negotiation skills and world history. Yet, they cannot get away with the neglected emotional intelligence which should be cultivated in order to be competent practitioners in politics. Otherwise, world politics wouldn't go further than a political pantomime of power struggle between the unsympathetic administrators in politics and the sufferers of the political hazards. The following table consists of some prompts for the potential candidates to experiment with in order to activate their emotional intelligence. If the potential candidates are able to come up with correct answers to the questions with 50% success rate, they should congratulate themselves on possessing an average emotional IQ which should qualify them to enter politics without much difficulty. If they score less than 50%, they shouldn't consider politics as a vocation before increasing their emotional IQ to the average 50% through looking at the Table of Mood, Attitude, Responsibility, Action (MARA, 2018) for some tips to reflect on.

Emotional Intelligence Checklist in Politics

Outfit	Life Style	Moral Integrity	Political Capability
How do you relate to unemployed people who can't afford to buy cloths cost more than £10 for an average shirt, trousers or raincoat? Your Answers 1. 2. 3.	How do you relate to people who live on a rented accommodation without any possibility of buying their 1st home during their life time? Your Answers 1. 2. 3.	How do you relate to people who feel demoralized for not being treated equal in education, at workplace and in their domestic environment as women employees and domestic providers such as mothers, spouses with disabled family members? Your Answers 1. 2. 3.	How do you resolve poverty at national level? What is your projected figure for eliminating local poverty during the next 5 years? Your Answers 1. 2. 3.
How do you relate to people who have got a limited spending power with the average budget of £200 for domestic appliances such as cooker, fridge and washing machine every five year? Your Answers 1. 2. 3.	How do you relate to people who have never taken vacation for longer than 15 years during their working life? Your Answers 1. 2. 3.	How do you relate to people who are deprived from all the privileges of the wealthy class such as private ownerships of accommodation, car, paid employment, qualifications, paid vacation and comfortable old age prospect with an adequate state retirement plan? Your Answers 1. 2. 3.	How do you resolve poverty on a global scale? What is your projected figure to eliminate global poverty during the next 5 years? Your Answers 1. 2. 3.

Table 1 Emotional Intelligence Checklist in Politics © Firdevs Dede

Mood, Attitude, Responsibility, Action (MARA, 2018) For Potential Candidates in Politics			
Mood	Attitude	Responsibility	Action
Monitoring current moods on a daily basis increases politicians' self-awareness about the level of intensive negative emotions for subjectivity such as anguish, regret, anger misery, revulsion, vulnerability, and apprehension.	Monitoring self-attitudes towards the unexpected public outcomes increases politicians' resilience and place them in a strong position to be less judgmental and more tactful for diplomatic relationships.	Identifying public responsibilities to citizens under difficult conditions is more rewarding than the less problematic times of the world history.	Prioritizing the essential actions in a positive and workable structure is more beneficial than not getting priorities right in the first place.

Table 2 Mood, Attitude, Responsibility, Action (MARA, 2018) © Firdevs Dede

How to stay objective in politics

I've been witnessing a historical dilemma between being part of EU and out of EU in British politics since 1983. Political parties are divided with different opinions about this issue in the UK. Not having a mutual understanding of the political problems led the politicians into a chaotic disorder which caused a division amongst British citizens after the EU referendum with the majority vote of Brexit result by 53.4% to 46.6% on 23 Jun 2016 (BBC News, 2016).

I've been listening to the views of the politicians and general public about what went wrong with the EU relationship and what caused the majority vote for Brexit. I could pick up the clues of the agonizing frustration coming from all sides by not being able to agree with the underlying causes of the past and current problems. I assume this is only possible within a democratic platform as everyone's opinion is consulted on how they perceived the confusion, despair, joy as well as relief they've been experiencing even with the uncertainty of not knowing what will happen within a two-year period in terms of the UK economy. Each chaos brings us to the breaking point where there will be an agreement on what needs to be done in order to overcome uncertainties. When we think about the life on the whole, who could possibly give any guarantee for definitive certainty even for a short time? In politics, nothing could be 100% certain as every single day brings its own challenges, doubts with unpredictable events such as natural disasters, famine, genocide, ethnic cleansing, civil wars, terrorism and epidemics. We all live in a century which has been constantly causing all forms of dilemmas in human life; most of the time, the ordinary citizens unable to control the destiny of the world economy let alone their own lives. What happens if we get worried too much about the unpredictable nature of domestic and world economy? Would the irrational worry enable us to enjoy the current time with its unpredictable nature? Supposing we are going to face irrecoverable disasters in politics and economics, would worrying for the disastrous outcome prevent us from facing our destiny in any way? The obvious answer is no.

If there is going to be a natural disaster, we don't have any power to stop it. Yet, we have got an extra ordinary creative power to bear the consequences of all the disastrous circumstances without losing our optimism for survival. We could only do our best to overcome all the unpleasant happenings in life when we keep calm and proportioned with rational judgements on our decisions to choose the best option with our own consciousness rather than being imposed on us by others. I offer Business Wellbeing Coaching to the individuals who find it difficult to stay objective when they face personal, economic, social and political problems. Business Wellbeing Coaching strategies enable clients to be in charge of their objectivity without being sidetracked by negative emotions.

History shouldn't repeat itself!

When I was writing this book, there were so many political conflicts taking place all over the world. Eid celebration arrived at the time Muslim population in Iraq had been experiencing violent attacks on the 1st day of Eid celebration in 2016 following the end of Ramadan which is one month fasting period for disciplining of body and spirit. Muslim community had been divided since 2003 when Iraq was invaded by the external forces which is a tragic outcome of Iraq war. I watched the media coverage on the Iraq Inquiry or known as the Chilcot Inquiry. The Chilcot Inquiry report consists of 12 volumes; it is 2.6 million words long which cost £767 with a 150-page executive summary is being published separately that cost £30 (BBC, 07 Jul 2016).

How the violation of mass destruction was legitimized by the politicians, who acted on impulse without taking into consideration of the long-term effects on human life has been still causing global and environmental hazards as well as economic disasters. Iraq was invaded against the millions of people's reaction which includes the non-violent 217 MPs in the House of Common in the UK in 2003.

> "The UK's participation was extremely contentious. A total of 179 British service personnel was killed in Iraq

> between 2003 and 2009, when British troops left Iraqi soil. Tens of thousands of Iraqi civilians died over the period, though estimates vary considerably."

> "The House of Commons authorized military action 72 hours before it took place but 217 MPs voted against, including 139 Labour MPs. Several members of the then Labour government, including former Foreign Secretary Robin Cook, resigned as a result. The weekend before the vote took place, millions of people took to the streets of London and other British cities to voice their opposition to military action."

BBC, 2016

History shouldn't repeat itself! Prevention is better than the last minute's violent interventions. It is possible to prevent the occurrence of the similar mass distractions around the world if only politicians keep remembering Sir John Chilcot's statement (2016) each time political violence steers outsiders to take violent actions against one nation or another.

> "The judgements about the severity of the threat posed by Iraq's weapons of a mass destruction - WMD - were presented with a certainty that was not justified. Despite explicit warnings, the consequences of the invasion were underestimated."

BBC, 2016

Politicians will benefit from BWC practice or Unity of Hexagon interactions before making important decisions during their political career to avoid getting things wrong with the majority of the victims are buried as the political errors of the past and the surviving casualties serving as the witnesses of the historical disasters like Iraqi orphan Ali Ismail Abbas, perhaps! When Ali's home was bombed at the age of 12 during the 2003 invasion in Iraq, Ali lost everything including his home, his family and his both arms. Ali must have lost his hope for a better future when his both arms blown off by a missile. An innocent Iraqi child of the horrific circumstances of the war searched for an answer to justify the unjustifiable act of the violent attack soon after being victimized.

> "Our house was just a poor shack. Why did they want to bomb us?"
>
> "It was midnight when the missile fell on us. My father, my mother and my brother died. My mother was five months pregnant."
>
> BBC (9th Apr 2013)

Ali was taught how to paint with his feet during his recovery period from the trauma of irrecoverable losses by his therapist Nafisa Kamal. I remember seeing some of his pictures in the newspapers and sharing with my OCR literacy students during the reading classes. Ali is in his late 20s now and he is married to his childhood friend. They are enjoying their parenthood with their miracle baby to prove God's mercy in the life of Iraqi survivors from the hopeless war zone. Ali challenges the war makers with the following question;

> "I wanted to be an army officer when I grow up but not anymore. Now I want to be a doctor - but how can I? I don't have hands."
>
> BBC (9th Apr 2013)

Unfortunately, remembering each war case with its tragedies doesn't prevent politicians from getting things wrong when politics is turned into a bloody victimization of the vulnerable civilians over and over again in the most brutal way throughout the centuries! If politicians are unable to resolve the problems through verbal interactions, missiles usually take over to destroy humanity without any negotiation of bloodless solutions. Let's learn to communicate with powerful words to diminish powerless violence against humanity for the sake of unity as God's creations. The famous quotes from the peaceful individuals speak louder when the topic of peace comes into our minds.

> *"An eye for an eye only ends up making the whole world blind."*
>
> **Mahatma Ghandi**

> *"If we have no peace, it is because we have forgotten that we belong to each other."*
>
> **Mother Teresa**

> *"Peace cannot be kept by force; it can only be achieved by understanding."*
>
> **Albert Einstein**

> "Where there is righteousness in the heart, there is beauty in the character. When there is beauty in the character, there is harmony in the home. When there is harmony in the home, there is order in the nation. When there is order in the nation, there is peace in the world."
>
> **A.P. J. Abdul Kalam**

I wish our warrior ancestors reflected on powerful words about peace with a mindful awareness daily to avoid violent reaction against all forms of injustice. Inner peace and world peace may only emerge once we work on our anger, hatred, inner distraction which requires conscious training of our body, mind and spirit with calming and peaceful words regularly. Please experiment with the spiritual exercises included here and share its positive impact on developing your unique spiritual ID with your fellow human beings by going beyond the formal religious practices and see how the external violence will be decreased eventually.

Code of ministerial practice in politics

How do politicians comply with Code of Practice in the democratic countries practicing certain political ideologies, such as the rule of law, human rights and equality? Is there any written code for politicians to follow as members of Cabinet or Parliament? Who is responsible to monitor each politician's actions either internally or globally in the Western world? What is the distinction between acceptable and unacceptable actions? Who decides what is appropriate or not? What happens when things go wrong in politics? What types of responses could remedy the chaotic situations based on improper code of practice? The above questions instantly activate citizens' curiosity to make enquiries about politicians' rights and wrongs each time the unfortunate individuals fall into the same vicious circle of Drama Triangle as a victim, a persecutor and a rescuer at the same time. The originator of Drama Triangle, Dr. Stephen Karpman introduced his concept 50 years ago. Karpman (1968) claimed that everyone has got the experience of complicated human relationships on a daily basis either through primary knowledge or secondary one by observing others' struggle during the unsuccessful communication process.

The unpleasant news broke out on the British media (BBC, Nov, 2017) when Priti Patel resigned as UK international development secretary due to the controversy over her unauthorized meetings with Israeli officials. The British Media (2017) interpreted the varying circumstances as "Rather than changing the minister, the Prime Minister has decided to change the ministerial code." Finally, Patel had to resign from her role as the situation got out of hands. Each comment from the officials, reporters and Patel had contributed to the dysfunctional interactions by accepting the scripted roles of a Drama Triangle which promoted emotions of righteousness, blame and fear amongst the individuals involved. There were winners and losers while the 'Political Drama Triangle' with unpredictable outcomes was proceeding itself.

Once we develop our spiritual identity alongside our body and mind experience, it gets a lot easier to treat each situation not only from a logical perspective but also ethical perspective in order to comprehend what is more appropriate and what is not. Not having an access to Code of Practice in politics shouldn't make much difference if we have already developed a spiritual consistency or ethical judgement in the event of complicated situations. Business Wellbeing Coach offers a new way of looking at the daily patterns of human relationships without projecting ourselves being victimized, persecuted or rescued in a trap of Drama Triangle at work, in education and politics. When we consciously develop our unique spiritual IDs, Drama Triangle replaces itself with Unity of Hexagons as each person's contribution is equally valued within the complex structure of hierarchies in any profession and politics within any society. The perspective of Drama Triangle could be shifted to Unity of Hexagons with the developed spiritual IDs. Then, each individual plays an equally important social role to increase the success of each organization. If we treat each organizational platform as a meaningful pattern of hexagons, everyone is allowed to become the creator of their pattern which grows into the wider picture of any hierarchical structure where there will be responsibilities of our duties rather than abusing of political power or misinterpretation of obscurities when they occur.

Loss of political integrity & power of resilience

The military-backed civilian government allowed the first openly contested election in Burma 25 years later of their oppressive power in 2015. On 13 Nov 2015, the political party named as National League for Democracy (NLD) secured two-thirds of the seats in parliament to secure a majority (BBC, 2016). The Rohingya minority group was the only ethnic group left with a worst-case scenario, which was to face ethnic cleansing in 2017.

When I was working with one of my MA students who was writing her thesis on the Rohingya people's struggle for survival, we discussed the political conflicts in Burma in a great length in 2015. I remember my student expressing her concern that if nobody took any positive action soon, the Rohingya minority group would be facing the horrific genocide in the near future. My student was correct in her prediction. In 2017, the tragic news about the Rohingya race including women and children who were raped and slaughtered by Myanmar army forces was on the news. The UN Refugee Agency reported that more than 600.000 Rohingya children, women and men have been forced to flee to Bangladesh escaping violence in Burma since August 2017.

The survivors of the legitimized mass murder left the country their ancestors settled down a century ago which is named as Myanmar and situated in the bordering pathway of India, Bangladesh, Shina, Laos and Thailand. According to the statistics, there are more than 100 ethnic groups living in the same area. However, the Rohingya minority group was the only ethnic group to be victimized by Myanmar authorities' brutality which denied their rights to a nationality in Myanmar and restricted their freedom of movement, access to education, healthcare, employment even to practice their religion and participate in public life. The irony is that Aung San Suu Kyi who became a legendary figure of defending human rights turned into a puppet figure of the hostile power she willingly represents by denying the cruel genocide taking place towards the Rohingya group in Myanmar.

Aung San Suu Kyi's courage attracted public attention when she was arrested in her home country in 1989 as she spent 15 years under house arrest. She awarded the Nobel Peace Prize which honored her as an international heroin associating her with historical icons such as Nelson Mandela, Kailash Satyarthi and Malala Yousafzai. Aung San Suu Kyi's essay titled *"Freedom from Fear"* was released for publication and received the 1990 Sakharov Prize for Freedom of Thought which was established in Dec 1988 by the European Parliament. In her book, Aung San Suu Kyi makes a rather astonishing remark as *"Fear of losing power corrupts those who wield it."* Yet, she is doing exactly the same thing which she criticized bluntly years ago. The well-known public figures who supported Aung San Suu Kyi during the time when she looked transparent & courageous started condemning her double standard while the Rohingya minority group was being attacked by the Myanmar army officials and she kept silent with her official title as a State Counsellor. Aung San Suu Kyi would have benefited if she was coached with the basic strategies of BWC. If Aung San Suu Kyi chose to be true to her starting point in politics with the same transparency not only to her own ethnic background but to other ethnic groups such as the Rohingya Muslims whose human dignity has been completely ruined by the corrupted Myanmar army officials' violence, she wouldn't receive public condemnation.

In contrast to Aung San Suu Kyi's cowardice attitude towards the genocide of the Rohingya Muslims in Myanmar with her agonizing silence at the age of 72, the young and brave Malala Yousafzai's dignity is admirable while she has been confronting not only her perpetrator Taliban from Pakistan but all the officials involved with violence from all sides. Malala's first speech on her 16th birthday at Harvard University (Sept 2013) displays her fearless courage to condemn all forms of threat against civil rights which denied Muslim girls' access to a well-balanced education system in her home country in Pakistan. Malala makes her statement with the following words:

"**When no one speaks and the whole world is silent, then, even one voice becomes powerful.**"

Malala's bravery extended further when she successfully challenged US President Barack Obama for his use of drone strikes in Pakistan in 2013. Malala shared the Nobel Peace Prize of 2014 with Kailash Satyarthi whose surname is interpreted as *Speaker of Truth*. Satyarthi advocates children's rights for a better life and fights against child exploitation including sexual abuse and sex trafficking. Satyarthi doesn't stay silent when there is a need for him to speak up. He stands up for the justice of the most vulnerable, weak and exploited. While the whole world and Aung San Suu Kyi ignored the sexual exploitation of the refugee Rohingya children without their biological parents to protect them in Bangladesh as the aftermath of the evil genocide took place in Myanmar, the honorable resistance of Kailash Satyarthi and Malala Yousafzai against injustice make a perfect sense to some of us who are able to differentiate between right and wrong through our mutual spiritual consciousness!

Corporate culture restricts disabled students' autonomy

I've been experiencing a political conflict between the short-sighted corporate providers' rigidity and the needs of my students who have been facing all forms of obstacles set for them within the academic institutions on their own. Some of the large and medium size supply teaching agencies caused problems with their rigid corporate culture mentality which neglects students' wellbeing. There is no room for negotiation. The most vulnerable disabled students' needs are underestimated as many agencies act in the most restrictive ways by reducing the students' visibility to numbers without considering their essential legal rights to be treated with respect for choosing what type of support they need and how they want to receive it e.g. face-to-face or distance learning. I have lost some of my disabled students with whom I had a very good working relationship due to the supply teaching agencies' inflexibility. When a dyslexic student was unable to attend his face-to-face support sessions, his request for distance learning was rejected while he was out of country on bereavement leave attending family funeral and couldn't postpone his deadline for the submission of his dissertation in the final year of his BA degree course.

Another negative experience is worth recording here that some of my final year students couldn't get their support sessions because the supply teaching agency asked me to stop delivering academic support to the students whose deadlines were negotiated with their course tutors and received further extension for the late submission of their final thesis. I remember having an initial session with one of my MA students before she flew to India to carry out her empirical research for two weeks over her summer vacation which delayed her theoretical assignment in 2015. I agreed to resume her support sessions when she returned to London. Upon her arrival, I provided her support tuition as agreed. She couldn't finish her theoretical research within a short time. She asked for another extension for the submission of her final dissertation and she secured the final extension successfully. During the critical time of her theoretical studies which she needed to gain intensive research skills, I received a notification from the supply teaching agency that the student's deadline for the completion of her academic study was over and my timesheet for teaching her couldn't be processed. I wrote to the agency and explained the situation the student was facing. The delay for an immediate response to my student's need caused the communication barrier. My MA student was left alone facing a sink or swim situation without receiving an academic lifejacket in the depth of academic ocean with so many academic conventions and jargons needed to be digested before submitting her dissertation. I assumed she was hurt and didn't understand the conflict I was facing under the inflexible working conditions while I was employed by the agency.

Despite my good will to decrease the certain inconveniences my adult dyslexic students were facing, I often found myself in a situation that I could not support DSA-funded students. Because of the restrictive practice of the corporate supply teaching agencies, some of my students suffered from unfair treatment when they needed to be supported, especially while they were facing unforeseeable personal circumstances that they didn't want to share with the faceless corporate administrators. Fairness became one-sided perspective during the mishandling of supply teaching agencies with an obscure restriction which made it impossible for me to support my students when they were granted with 30 hrs. support each academic year by the state.

The financial discrepancy is the most detrimental restriction specialist tutors/mentors are expected to face with a financial penalty when they are willing to accommodate their students' need within a flexible time-schedule such as 24/7 availability. The corporate supply teaching agencies can easily deduct specialist tutors/mentors' hourly rates; in some cases, they dismiss them by asking them not to provide the most needed service to their students in distress outside the 9 to 5 working pattern. There is a high level of uncertainty between the corporate supply teaching agencies and specialist tutors/mentors in terms of trust or a lack of it. The unfair treatment reduces specialist tutors/mentors' professional autonomy while they are working for corporate supply teaching agencies. Therefore, there is a need for an alternative solution which should free the disabled students and their specialist tutors/mentors for a better workable solution instead of being demoralized by the unworkable oppressive corporate cultures. BWC or Unity of Hexagons coaching strategies could be more applicable within the most rigid industries where clients' autonomy has been reduced to the bare minimum without giving them a chance to exercise their legal entitlements for freedom of choice. Dyslexic students will benefit from empathetic and flexible approach to their special needs in order to be accommodated without facing discrimination of bureaucratic obstacles.

Whose incompetence, disabled students or staff?

Each academic year brings its demands for the diagnosed dyslexic students to do better than previous year or face the challenges of an academic life in the first year without knowing how to follow certain procedures such as whom to contact for help within unwelcoming academic environment. It was the beginning of a new academic year; my home telephone rang. I was contacted by an undiagnosed dyslexic student in Sept 2017 as the undiagnosed student believes he is dyslexic and he expressed his need for academic study skills support. I've done a lot of research on his behalf in order to get this young undiagnosed student on a right track to find his whereabouts within the complicated systems of an academic life. I've been providing one-to-one academic study skills to dyslexic students for a long time in the UK; yet, I still find it difficult to reach the right person to get undiagnosed dyslexic students diagnosed in the absence of an adequate provision at some educational establishments. I contacted several people for help. Some provided valuable information, some didn't pay much attention to my enquiries. I jotted down the details of the most helpful people for an intention of using them as part of my referral system whenever necessary. In the likelihood of another call from undiagnosed dyslexic students, I will be able to refer them on to the relevant people so that they will be diagnosed which will enable them to be recognized as dyslexic students and have an access to their disabled students allowance within a reasonable timeframe.

If the academic system doesn't recognize dyslexic students' visibility without sufficient evidence which can only be provided with a full diagnostic report, they are more likely to be treated like a failure from the right beginning to the end of their academic studies. Even having a full diagnostic report of their difficulties doesn't guarantee that dyslexic students would be accommodated within academic establishments as I met many dyslexic students who face biased academics' discrimination because of their hidden disabilities. I feel that academics should receive pedagogical and andragogical training to differentiate dyslexic students' cognitive profile well enough so that they will adjust their delivery methods for their subject specific areas. Otherwise, dyslexic students' experience of academic life cannot go beyond painful memories of being placed in a disadvantaged situation while they are turned into a failure by some academics' errors which ignore dyslexic students' needs for dyslexia-friendly teaching methods.

How could an academic staff without any hidden disability empathize with dyslexic students' weaknesses and strengths? The goodwill of the academic staff is the core spiritual value for selfless commitment to dyslexic students' wellbeing. How can non-dyslexic academics adopt the dyslexia-friendly teaching methods which won't intimidate dyslexic students? Teaching dyslexic adults shouldn't be complicated! However, it takes time to master the skills of empathic teaching. Through practice, any academic should be able to replace the rigid teaching methods such as traditional ways of lecture delivery with more empathic approaches such as discussions. Accepting and understanding of dyslexic students' cognitive profile is essential for meaningful interactions without being judgmental about dyslexic students' weaknesses. Dyslexia-friendly teaching methods encourage dyslexic students to work on their strengths which provide a sufficient answer for some dyslexic students' learning preferences.

Social media has been bombarded with the adverts and posts which promise how to increase earning capacity of freelance professionals with commercial marketing strategies. In my view, social media should be used as a platform for dyslexic students and independent support providers who try to function outside corporate supply teaching agencies so that it will be easier to be connected without facing gatekeepers' discrimination. Unfortunately, there is not a legitimate platform between the independent freelance support providers and DSA-funded dyslexic students who are eligible for one-to-one specialist study skills tuition. Dyslexic students are bullied to use the large and medium corporate type supply teaching agencies only instead of receiving the list of independent freelance support providers like myself. I was astonished to learn that students experiencing anxiety, panic attack and chronic depression were referred to their GPs or emergency services at hospitals on a university website. Supposing a student with depression or anxiety disorder went to emergency service of the nearest hospital, they wouldn't be able to get effective interactions with a qualified person on a regular basis. I was working with a student who suffered from acute depression and missed all his deadlines as a result of his depression. I suggested him to contact the wellbeing officer at his university and get a letter of confirmation for his inability to focus on his assignments with the aim of getting an extension for his overdue assignments instead of being asked to leave the university. The young depressed student was told by the wellbeing officer that there wasn't any facility to accommodate his need at university and he was left alone without any referral system of any kind and without knowing what to do next.

Another student of mine was going through traumatic experience of loss in her life while she was doing her postgraduate degree in teaching. The dyslexic learner lost her aunt from cancer; her mother was hospitalized as a cancer patient and her father died from a heart attack. These tragedies happened within short intervals less than a year. She had to cope with all her bereavements while she was at her school placement as a trainee teacher. Her mentor at school placement didn't show any understanding of the difficulties she was facing at that time. He asked her to leave the school placement on the grounds of finding her incompetent. She was heartbroken. She grieved not only for her loved ones she lost but the loss of her potential teaching career which she was looking forward to. Strangely enough, the useless academics turned their back on this young & talented student by refusing to find her another school placement. The disability team didn't prevent the unfairness of her expulsion from teaching profession. The trainee teacher was asked to leave her teaching training without support from the academics. The disability team of the university failed to act as a mediator between the student and the university to resolve the discriminative nature of expulsion. The demoralized trainee teacher was feeling penalized for the ill-fated circumstances created by the academics and her mentor at school placement. I was unable to take up her case within the boundary of my role as a specialist tutor working for a multinational corporate supply teaching agency at that time.

These kinds of discriminative treatments occur frequently within the unfair academic systems with biased academics who are unable to investigate the real reasons behind students' poor performance. When I was working for an agency which limited my involvement with my students' wellbeing; I couldn't act as her advocate and lessen the negative consequences of the selfish individuals' involvement with the destructive actions of ruining a bright student's potential career. I felt powerless for not being able to reduce the most damaging barriers some of my talented dyslexic students had to face during their academic studies. I decided to write this book in order to increase the visibility of some of my dyslexic students' negative experiences with a strong hope for a positive change which should include treating disabled students fairly by the academics, need assessors and disability provision in FE and HE in the UK and beyond.

While I was working as an external provider for the well-known universities in London, I was able to observe the negative effects of the internal oppression adult dyslexic students were suffering from. Some of the disability team members, academics and need assessors with racial, sexual, cultural biases treated dyslexic academic students with contempt. Students' freedom of choice for selecting their external providers was completely taken away from them. Dyslexic students weren't allowed to make their own choices for the mode of delivery e.g. face-to-face or remote; how often they wanted to see their support tutors and what strategies they felt beneficial for them to learn. The whole disability provision within the Student Loan Company (SLC) and universities' internal disability advisors restricts academic students' rights to be treated impartially.

Some of the aggressive disability advisors threaten dyslexic students with the withdrawal of their disability student allowance if they requested seeing DSA-QAG registered external specialist tutors/mentors working independently. Dyslexic academic students are still forced to use large or medium size corporate supply teaching agencies who are favored by disability advisers and need assessors. The majority of the dyslexic students are systematically harassed for requesting individual support tutors registered with DSA-QAG in HE and FE in the UK. The distressed dyslexic students are abused by disability teams, need assessors and corporate agencies rather than being empowered.

The author, Paula Freire was jailed for his attempts to advance the educational movement in Brazil during the time the military coup took over the government in 1964. Freire's book titled *"Pedagogy of the Oppressed"* is treated as a classic text of critical pedagogy today and sold a million copies. Paula Freire describes how the oppressed and oppressor seen together in his book as follows:

> *"Every prescription represents the imposition of one individual's choice upon another, transforming the consciousness of the person prescribed to into one that conforms with the prescriber's consciousness. Thus, the behavior of the oppressed is a prescribed behavior, following as it does the guidelines of the oppressor."*
>
> **Paula Freire, 1968**

I remember my misfortune experiencing the non-stop episodes of oppression I faced when I encouraged my dyslexic students to stand up for their legal entitlements to be treated fairly. Twenty of my dyslexic students were taken away from me by the forceful intrusion of the aggressive disability teams at two different universities in London. Some of the need assessors didn't recommend me when my returning students chose me as their support tutor during their studies for their second or third degrees. I cannot see the motive behind the disability provision's discrimination against me and my dyslexic students.

I am registered with the HMRC in the UK; I pay Professional Indemnity Insurance annually; I am registered with DSA-QAG and Patoss. The subscriptions of my membership to professional organizations cost me a small fortune. Yet, I am not treated as equal as large and medium size corporate supply teaching agencies. There isn't any valid reason why the disability provision within the Student Loan Company (SLC) discriminated me. I was bullied and threatened by some of the disability teams. While I was assisting one of my dyslexic students in the assistive technology center (ATC) which is originally designated for dyslexic students' study area, the senior librarian at a university in London threatened me to leave the ATC in front of my adult dyslexic student who is a professional art curator. We were forced to leave the ATC and moved to the noisy student café to find an alternative solution urgently. I suggested my MA student home tuition since I wasn't able to enter ATC and library under the dictatorship of the senior librarian. The dyslexic student was happy to take up home tuition. Unfortunately, the supply teaching agency didn't allow me to deliver home tuition to my MA student despite the fact that I used to deliver home tuition to several dyslexic students previously while I was working for the same supply teaching agency for longer than a year. My dyslexic student was left alone without being able to have an access to her support tuition either at university or in her home during the critical time of having overdue submission date for her dissertation.

The senior librarian became a nuisance following me everywhere in the library and bullying me to leave the library eventually. The offensive senior librarian prevented me from entering the university library which didn't make any sense to me and my dyslexic students as I was issued a staff library pass in the capacity of a support tutor for dyslexic students which allowed me to enter the library for providing support to dyslexic students initially. The pass was issued to me by the disability team of the university. I could have taken the senior librarian to court for her discriminative harassment as all the external support tutors were allowed to enter the library except me. I was penalized by the librarian aggressive political fallacy. Ironically enough, I made enquiries about PhD registration at the same university prior to my employment as an external staff. After experiencing the systematic bullying tactic of the senior librarian, I would never consider to pursue PhD research at the same university any longer. I avoid attending cultural events taking place there when I occasionally receive an invitation for opening views of art exhibitions as the hostile librarian permanently stays the forefront face of the university in my subconscious.

Some supply teaching agencies ripped me off and didn't pay me what they owed me for the support tuitions I delivered to my dyslexic students. Despite the non-stop discrimination took place against me and my dyslexic students, I continued tutoring, mentoring and coaching dyslexic students in HE/FE since 2012. I accumulated the best memories of being trusted and respected by some of my dyslexic students over the years. When I reflect on my memories within the hostile environment of the academic establishments, I identify the biased academics' underestimation of my contribution to dyslexic students' wellbeing. It is not easy for me to forgive the offensive disability provision with discriminative attitude and political conspiracies. It is like facing a commercial espionage organized by unethical competitors in disability provision year in and year out. A union protecting academic lecturers' employment rights didn't protect my legal right when I turned to them for support. I was left on my own devices as an employee. The incompetent solicitor overcharged me for looking at my case without offering a valid resolution to the systematic political harassment I faced in 2014. Disabled students' hidden disability was constantly ignored by the unsympathetic disability advisors, need assessors and corporate agencies. My input as a specialist tutor/mentor was taken for granted. When I attended the graduation ceremony to share one of my dyslexic students' achievement, there wasn't any academic recognizing my contribution to the success of some of my dyslexic students I supported over the years. I took my invisibility with humility when I gave a big applause to the privileged internal academic staff praised by the university governors during the graduation ceremony. Everything counts in education including praises and exclusions for reflection years later. I've highlighted some important points to be considered by the academics who find it difficult to teach disabled students in HE/FE.

Mood, Attitude, Responsibility, Action (MARA, 2018) Teaching Competence in HE/FE			
Mood	**Attitude**	**Responsibility**	**Action**
Monitoring MOODS daily increases self-awareness about the level of intensive negative emotions of subjectivity such as revulsion, anger and intolerance towards disabled students. How do you monitor your mood while you are teaching disabled students? Please jot down your answers. 1. 2. 3.	Monitoring ATTITUDES towards disabled students' need for understanding and non-judgmental approach is better than dismissing them for their errors they make beyond their deliberate intention. Please remember it isn't dyslexic students' fault to make errors such as spelling mistakes, forming ungrammatical sentences and not being able to meet deadlines. How do you monitor your attitudes towards disabled students' errors? Please jot down your answers. 1. 2. 3.	Identifying teaching RESPONSIBILITIES to disabled students who are facing hardship is more rewarding than labelling them as failures. Please remember teachers FAIL themselves each time they fail their students. What are your responsibilities to the disabled students who face hardship during their studies such as bereavement, being diagnosed with life-threatening diseases, loss of job, divorce, miscarriage, bad debt and depression? Please jot down your answers. 1. 2. 3.	Developing SENSITIVITY to decide what actions are considered positive and workable not only within the short-term but in the long-term is the basis of EFFECTIVE teaching practice. How do you identify your long-term objectives for positive actions in your teaching career which should include disabled students? Please jot down your answers. 1. 2. 3.

Table 3 Teaching Competence (MARA, 2018) © Firdevs Dede

All genuine prayers are valid within cross-cultural context

At the age of 25, I was confronted by the boundaries of spiritual values on cross cultural platform in a residential home for elderly women in London. I was connected to the elderly residents from various spiritual backgrounds through compassion and courtesy while I was working there in the early 1980s. I listened to the fragile residents' daily worries during my befriending visits. I made a very good friend with one of the residents. The strong bond with her lasted until she passed away which was soon after my both parents' departure in the late 1990s. When I attended my old friend's funeral in a church in north London, I sobbed not only for the loss of a good friend but loss of my own parents as all my losses came one after another.

I met a terminally ill resident in the residential home in 1983. Years later, I still remember our conversation took place while I was dusting and tidying up her room as a Community Service Volunteer (CSV).

> 'I suffer from incurable type of cancer. I'm dying. Could you pray for me?'

'Of course, I'd pray for you. Please don't worry. No one knows for how long we've got in this life. Our life depends on God's Grace.'

'You're right, actually. But, I won't last long.'

'Are you afraid of dying?'

'I don't want to die. Would you pray for me?'

'I'd pray for you.'

'What is your faith?'

'I was born in Moslem culture. I respect all the religions.'

'I see.'

It didn't feel a right attitude to mask my religious background for the sake of comforting the elderly resident. After revealing my religious background, the hope in the eyes of the elderly resident faded away as though my prayers had no spiritual value in her Christian world. I was saddened by the reality that I took away the dying person's hope she placed in me. The subtle differences between religious interpretations of the Almighty didn't block my spiritual connection to the faithful individuals from different spiritual backgrounds as I believe we were all created by the same Divine Creator. Nevertheless, I felt that it was unacceptable for the terminally ill elderly resident to be comforted by my prayers while she was facing her mortality in a residential home on her own.

In 2002, I was blessed with a class of my own in London, while I was working with my ESOL students from multi-faith backgrounds. The best experience of spiritual richness increased my job satisfaction in my multi-cultural ESOL classes as all my students spiritually related to me without feeling any boundary of their formal spiritual identity. We had a spiritually fulfilling time together when we had a good laugh during the happy moments of realization; how close we were regardless different rituals of religious practices we all belonged to. We shared spiritual anecdotes. The spiritual wisdom united us by accepting our spiritual uniqueness. We celebrated our similarities as well as our differences. We understood one another better than reading different interpretation of spiritual doctrines written by scholars.

In 2012, I wanted to do an MA in Religion and Philosophy at a university where multi faith practices from Judaism, Christianity to Islam were offered on the same platform with the representors of each religion. Despite my expectation of finding a place with the mutual understanding of various faiths, the course lecturers chose to introduce us the philosophers who disregarded the faith systems altogether. I felt there was no point in learning the nihilist philosophers who dismissed the spiritual need of modern human beings when I wanted to be reassured by the lecturers that all the genuine prayers were valid. I left the course with disappointment as I couldn't risk my spiritual identity which was too precious to lose within the obscure syllabus of delivery in HE.

Years later, I still believe that all genuine prayers have got a spiritual value within the cross-cultural context as we share our common ancestors Adam and Eve. Even my Buddhist and Hindu students shared their prayers with me. No matter, what faith we all practice, we all have spiritual identity which gives us a spiritual license to include the whole humanity and animals in our spiritual meditations on our daily prayers. The spiritual currency of each genuine prayer is equally valuable to heal us spiritually which increases our wellbeing gradually as we become more fulfilled and happier than the times lost without spiritual meditation among the materialistic world of consumerism.

One day, while I was feeding birds, swans, ducks, geese and squirrels in a local park, I met a Buddhist Vietnamese lady, who is a regular visitor of our mutual animal friends. The spark in her eyes is remarkable at the time she feeds the animals with spiritual fulfilment. Once we stopped and talked to each other longer than usual greetings. She told me how strongly she was related to the animals in the park. According to her spiritual belief system, all the animals have spirits and they need to be fed by us. The Vietnamese grandmother revealed that she feels so good each time she feeds the animals. If she misses out on a feeding day, she feels very sad. How good it is to meet a fellow human being with spiritual connection to our mutual animal friends! Connecting to our environment and the wild animals at a spiritual level increase our wellbeing enormously. After all, the animals like us were created by our Divine Creator.

On 23 Dec 2017, there was a terrible fire at London Zoo; the four meerkats were assumed to be killed during the fire (BBC, Dec 2017). The 70 firefighters couldn't save all the animals. I felt the pain when I heard the tragic circumstances of the zoo animals as I believe animals' life is sacred and precious like other creations of our Creator. I often include wild animals and environment alongside human beings in my prayers to be protected by our Creator. None of us could function in an environment without the wildlife such as animals, plants, trees, streams, lakes, rivers, waterfalls, coastlines, oceans, mountains and valleys. Human beings are part of the whole picture our Creator created and we would be incomplete without the wildlife as the extension of our ecosystem. If our ecosystem is damaged or neglected by uncaring human destructions, we become less connected to our healing human nature as there will be a disconnection with our planet of mother earth and its natural essences which include the wildlife and its vegetations. I remember seeing the healthy ancient trees' disappearance within my living environment by the destructive actions of ecologically insensitive human beings. Each time a healthy tree is destroyed, I feel the pain of its loss in my whole body. I pray that humanity becomes more sensitive to our ecological system and our ecological wellbeing. I am sure all the prayers will be accepted if the prayers are based on good intentions which will heal us all and protect our environments from inhuman destructions. The Business Wellbeing Coach works with everyone from different religious practices and makes them comfortable within a welcoming environment in which the participants are all valued for their contribution to the spiritual community of good causes.

Wellbeing investment plan is better than financial investment plan

I was interrupted by a sudden telephone call which I wasn't expecting. An unwanted caller wasted my time by interrupting me with unpleasant questions about my financial investment plan. I cut the talk short as I sensed that the caller was interested in his own financial benefit rather than mine by cheating me over the phone. I remembered hearing so many senior citizens were misled by investment scams. Unlucky retired people lost their lifelong savings within minutes by transferring their savings on to the scam companies accounts via telephone persuasion technique.

After putting the phone down, I started reflecting on the scam companies who tried to deceived me with so many financial investment scams which sounded like genuine investment each time they approached me with their tricks and aggressive selling tactics. I realized that I would have been wiser not to take an action when I was distracted by the scam companies' dishonesty. I could have saved my precious time, money and energy which could have been invested in my physical, mental and spiritual wellbeing instead. I could have spent the wasted money I lost through scam investment plans on a well-deserved holiday treat within a pleasant environment which could have made a positive impact on my wellbeing's sustainability in the long run.

We all need to look after ourselves while we are facing uncertainties in life. There is no guarantee for any of us to have a longitudinal extension of life span in any case. Supposing we are blessed with a blissful longevity, investing in our wellbeing should be the best investment any individual could possibly make through spending a pleasant and meaningful time outside monotonous working patterns. We all deserve a well-planned investment plan to give us a decent break for revitalizing ourselves within a new environment which should take off our minds from daily worries of keeping our job without being redundant; making a career change; setting up another business or doing a degree to improve our earning capacity. All those financial investment plans might wait for a while but we cannot ignore the best investment plan in our physical, emotional and spiritual wellbeing. Let's consider the grim reality, in the case of becoming the wealthiest person in the world but not having enough time to enjoy a decent meal; a restful goodnight sleep; a fresh air to breath and an unpolluted environment to take a delight in. What is the use of all our financial investment if it doesn't enhance our wellbeing? At a mature age, my priorities have been shifted from financial investment to personal wellbeing investment. I don't see any benefit of having financial investment without having a quality of life. My first priority is to invest in my wellbeing by taking some time off for recharging my body, mind and spirit which benefits me more than any financial investment plan I was persuaded to take up by scam companies so far. The Business Well Being Coach explores the human emotions such as how to be happier, fitter and more satisfied with our personal and professional lives rather than focusing on useless financial investment plans. Earning a living is one thing; knowing how to live our life is another. We need to get the balance right without overstretching our emotional resources. We'll be wiser to live our lives without reaching our breaking point which might not give us any turning point to catch up with what we have already lost e.g. our youth and/or our health. Our life with genuine priorities for our wellbeing cannot be postponed for another decade or so. The present time is the most important value. We could be better off if we capitalize on present time without ignoring our vital priorities for a renewal of our human energy within our limited lifespan peacefully. Tomorrow might be too late for us all to regain our health once we are burned out completely.

I remember the life-long struggle of three decades a friend of mine experienced. He saved money for the rainy days to have a comfortable retirement with his family. The bank went into liquidation. He lost all his life-long saving after retirement. He had no choice but to work very hard to supplement his insufficient state pension until the last two years of his time. His health declined so rapidly; he became bed-ridden without any energy to get out of his bed to go for a short walk. It was too late for him to regain his strength. Sadly, I heard that he passed away after a year struggle with the failing health when he was barely 70 years old. He didn't have a quality of life during the three decades I have known him and his family. His family wished that he spent all his savings when he was alive for a better life style. I wished the same for my both parents who didn't have a quality of life when they were constantly saving for the rainy days neglecting their own needs for a regular holiday treat.

Unfortunately, we do not know the length of time we have on this earth. There is always a constant worry about the future which we cannot predict. We are advised to save regularly in order to ease our daily survival at a mature age. We get carried away by the non-stop saving plans for a better future during our working life. When we reach our breaking point, it is too late to regain our youth and start all over again to fulfil our ambition for a well-deserved vacation. There isn't even enough time to say goodbye to our friends when our time is up for another journey in eternity. Let's make the most of our life whatever is left over. There is no need for us to be too cautious to save money for retirement only! Occupying our minds with investment plans isn't worth it in the expense of neglecting our wellbeing. Taking a regular, well-deserved quality of time is the best investment for the young and the old at the same time!

Our life experiences are confined between time and space

Our mortality is limited as the average life expectancy at birth of the global population didn't exceed longer than 71.4 years (GHO, 2015). We need to think twice each time we make an important decision to commit ourselves to long-term plan. Is it necessary to commit ourselves to a 20-years mortgage plan when we already reached our late 50s knowing that we might be in heaven by the time we reach our 70s? Is there any way we could find a short-term solution to our long-term problems such as homelessness, struggling with an insecure job prospect and purchasing a holiday package 6 month ahead of our vacation?

When I was in my early 20s I made long-term plans, which exceeded the limited life expectancy of a mortal human being. I've seen people with the similar attitude to time and space. Unfortunately, they couldn't even reach the average life-span and passed away in their early 40s. Time became the most precious commodity for me when I hit my 50; I made use of my last 8 years with delightful memories since 2010. While I was pondering around how I could reward myself for all the hard work I carried out during the period between 2016 and 2017 including writing this book in my spare time since 2015, I came across a substantial discount for Mediterranean Cruise. I made my decision instantly and took up the unique opportunity immediately with the intention of investing in my wellbeing. I took a week off between 11 Dec 2017 and 18 Dec 2017. Despite the fact that weather was rainy and I ended up getting wet when I was strolling in some of the cities in Europe, the voyage made a positive impact on my physical, mental and spiritual wellbeing. Additionally, I had the experience of how it felt to be on a cruise ship for a week enjoying splendid breakfasts on the deck 10 overlooking the sea view with the pleasant feeling of 'I made it at last!' I was fed regularly for three times a day. There was no need to worry about what to eat at meal times on cruise as oppose to my daily routine of creating time to cook for myself between work commitments e.g. teaching, coaching, mentoring students and meeting deadline for submission of my manuscripts in London. I could sleep long hours in my cabin room without any destruction of emails, phone calls and text messages. There was no commitment to anything apart from recharging my battery which I needed more than anything else. For me it was more than a photography research trip. I called my experience as Continuous Professional Development training as I could observe 4000 passengers' responses to delicious choices of healthy food, pleasant space, extravagant time to occupy with and their interactions with one another as well as with me. Some of the passengers were able bodied; some of them were disabled; some of them were young and some of them were elderly. The vital aspect of the experience was that there was no common language to communicate with. Most of the time, there was a language barrier which was resolved with an inventive sign language and our good intention to understand one another's messages without a common official language. I was pleased that I returned to London with pleasant memories of communication process from the first cruise experience.

I remember attending useless Continuous Professional Development (CPD) training throughout my professional careers in teaching, coaching and mentoring. Sometimes, my CPD training was paid by my employers. Regrettably, I usually received only little or no value out of the innumerous training programs I attended since 2002. I wasn't even given any certification of being on CPD training most of the time. I was disillusioned with the CPD training delivered for the sake of it without receiving any professional satisfaction of achieving anything concrete at the end. I am rather skeptical about CPD training without benefiting participants as practical experience; theoretical knowledge is limited to enhance anyone's professional development let alone their personal wellbeing. I prefer being in charge of my CPD. I benefit from the carefully selected meaningful CPDs physically, mentally and spiritually which provide long-term vivid memories for me to reflect on and write about them as I am sharing some of the latest CPD experiences with my readers in this book and on social media with my followers. Business Wellbeing Coach equips clients with a purposeful questioning technique which enables them to assess every action they take in their lives including attending CPD training. Moreover, BWC helps clients to identify the benefits of CPD to their whole wellbeing which is a combination of body, mind and spirit without limiting ourselves to a specific career pattern only. We need to be able to tick all the boxes related to our wellbeing each time we attend any training for continuous professional development.

Originality is misunderstood without any criteria for it

Have you ever thought about what it means to have an original idea? Have you looked at your own life and asked what makes your life more original than others? How do we know the thought process or activity we're occupied with is original? How well are we equipped to spot the originality? What makes us to be in tune with lateral thinking process? The majority of academic people are confused about the concept of originality. The 90% of academic educators experience a lack of originality in their delivery of theoretical lectures. The majority of academics usually are unable to know how to combine their practices with the unoriginal theories of the past centuries. The most stubborn unoriginal academics usually fail the most original work submitted by creative students as they reward the unoriginal assignments which are classified to fit the criteria they set for students to fulfil.

Many people lead a life style without any originality like unoriginal academics' banality of teaching methods within the stifling academic systems of modernity. The same patterns of daily life and holiday plans of average person occur for years which do not differ than the patterns of next-door neighbors, relatives or friends within their circle. The outfits are turned into some kind of uniform which appeal to the majority of the 21st century consumers under the dictation of the concept called fashion that means representation of all the same style from the same era. Most of us are influenced by the commercial adverts which shape our buying habits. Even human reactions to certain events lost their originality. The whole humanity became the product of the same factory with the same functioning skills, thinking style, world view, short-term, and long-term goals. No one looks different than you met last year, the year before or years ago. Everyone acts in the same manner with the same patterns of life style. Even the common celebrations of important days such as New Year celebrations for Christians, Moslems or Chinese repeat themselves in the same way as it has been happening years ago. Humanity suffers from a lack of originality. The trouble is no one admits this unpleasant reality even to themselves. Days, months, years go around the circle without any difference from yesterday. In the meantime, children start growing up by following the patterns of their parents and grand-parents. They become the product of their circumstances without questioning the non-stop repetition of their yesterdays. Nothing is more fulfilling or less boring than yesterday's human relationships. The whole concept of being human being blurs its meaningful originality which could have made life worth living.

I was thinking to suggest what needs to be focused in Business Wellbeing Coach and what needs to be avoided in order to increase creativity in my self-help book here. Then, I thought this would go against the nature of originality or lateral thinking itself. If I formulate what needs to be done or avoided in terms of originality in education, politics, life, at work, my formula might be taken as a replicable pattern of creativity, which could ruin the concept of originality and won't work for everyone and all the time. That's why Business Wellbeing Coaching

(BWC) only works instantly and depends on the two people's responses to each other's communication process. Coach and client experience the lateral thinking during the coaching process. Each coaching session is unique and coaching techniques can't be replicated even the circumstances might be prepared to resemble the repetition exactly the same way it took a month ago. It's like being once at one place and at one time only. You won't be at the same place at the same time you had been yesterday, a month ago and a year ago. Business Wellbeing Coach and client experience the interaction each time they meet with an originality of their natural responses to each other's communication process. That is why there won't be a list of questions to train Business Wellbeing Coach to replicate the best practice. A technique of prompting has to be originated by Business Wellbeing Coach each time they meet their different clients under different circumstances. There isn't a set of patterns to fit every purpose or everyone's need promising to get the same results. In reality, everyone has been treated as an autonomous participant of the unrepeatable interactions each time Business Wellbeing Coach interacts with a new client or the existing client over the fluctuating time and space. Business Wellbeing strategies are not replicable. That's why it is original and it differs from any other coaching techniques which are claimed to be replicable.

Breaking glass ceilings doesn't mean breaking cultural inequalities

I have been producing my artwork, photography, artefact and literature since 1983 in the UK. I've contacted a few public gallery spaces to contribute to the evolutional developments of British Culture and Ethnic Identities such as the National Poetry Library in Southbank; Royal Society of Literature in London; Brunel Museum in Rotherhithe; Café Gallery in Bermondsey; Swiss Cottage Library Gallery and DACS' gallery for my second solo exhibition with poetry recital and book reading. I did not get any positive response to all my attempts to hire a public space and reach the general public during the last three decades. Just recently, I had a vague hope that I might be able to break the cultural barriers with the help of the new director, Sandeep Mahal, who was appointed in 2016 to make a positive impact on the residents and visitors in Nottingham which is recognized as UNESCO City of Literature. Charlotte Anscombe (Nottingham University, 2015) shared the good news in her blog by quoting from the UNESCO Director, Irina Bokova in Paris about the importance of diversity as follows:

"I would like to recognize many new cities and their countries that are enriching the network with their diversity."

Charlotte Anscombe, 2015

What a good intension in theory! However, I'm sceptical about its practicality at least for myself as I am treated like an outsider of literature and visual art festivals in the UK. I received a plenty of rejections when I approached a relevant person or the people to be included as a producer but not only a consumer of literature and visual arts. Funnily enough, I did not give up on my hope to be recognised for my contribution to the British Culture as a productive member of the world literature and visual arts; I sent Sandeep Mahal the following email on 30/Nov/2017.

> Hello Sandeep,
>
> I hope you've been doing very well with your new role as a director of Nottingham UNESCO City of Literature since Sept 2016.
>
> I would like to make enquiries about the scope of your role. Would you include authors outside Nottingham for your literature projects? If it is so, please let me know how I should contribute to Literature World of Nottingham as a published Turkish/British author living and working in London since 1983. Thanks. Have a good day!
>
> Kind regards,
> Firdevs Dede

I wasn't surprised when Sandeep Mahal didn't respond to my request to be heard as an author with an academic background serving academic and non-academic audience from diverse backgrounds in the UK since 1983. While there was a prolong delay to my query, I was fully prepared for an apological rejection with the similar excuses of the letters I received from various officials previously. Instead, Sandeep Mahal chose to ignore my enquiry completely. I felt sorry for Mahal. She may be a successful director by including only politically motivated high-profile women to perform on her cultural platform but excluding me; ignoring my ethnicity that certainly neglects diversity. I remember discussing the cultural barriers some of the black women historians faced centuries ago with one of my BA students who was doing research for her assignment on black women academics such as Anna Julia Cooper who became the first African American woman achieving her PhD at the age of 66 at the University of Paris, Sorbonne in 1925. The following quote from Professor Dagbovie (2004) unmasks the various discriminations the black women historians had experienced.

> *"From the 1890s through the first half of the 20th century, black women historians overcame a different set of barriers than their male counterparts in earning their doctorates, publishing, securing employment, receiving professorial promotions, and gaining respect in academia."*

Prof. Pero Gaglo Dagbovie, 2004

Some black women historians from the 1890s to the 1930s took up fiction writing as it looked less threatening to the oppressive political systems; their professional knowledge had been masked in their novels. Nevertheless, the black women historians did not get an academic recognition for their literature work from politically discriminative academic circles. In the 21th century, I am ignored in the similar fashion black women historians were ignored in the 20th century. How irrational it is to divide the mainstream culture into subcultures of the politically motivated women writers and not offering any neutral cultural space for the women authors from ethnic minorities who stayed outside the political arena of destructive divisions for a very good reason. Funders of visual arts exhibitions and literature events cannot afford to discriminate neutral creators/producers under the ideological favouritism; it is unfair to reward the politically motivated women writers, visual artists and exclude the women writers whose intension is to break the barriers to free independent producers from the political oppression of any kind within art communities of our global village. Opportunities should be offered to everyone but not only to politically charged women within visual arts and literature circles. Removing cultural snobbery in decision making process for funding may provide a multi-cultural platform for all producers to take part without being discriminated against their political or non-political approaches.

I appreciate how Laura Eliza Wilkes (1871-1922), the public-school teacher felt when her request for an acknowledgement of her literature achievement didn't receive any response from the main culture. I am in the same boat without receiving sufficient attention from the hostile academics, literature circles, administrators of public art galleries/public museums in the UK longer than three decades. In his research outcomes, Professor Dagbovie evidenced Wilkes's concern about the unfair denial of the contribution the Black Women Authors made to the mainstream culture. When Wilkes submitted her work titled *Missing Pages in American History, Revealing the Services of Negroes in the Early Wars of America to* Carter G. Woodson, Wilkes's work was not reviewed in the journal of Negro History as cited in Dagbovie (2004), Black Women Historians, p.248.

"I submitted my work to you as soon as it came from the press and yet for some reason it has not received the courtesy, I had every right to expect for it."
Laura Eliza Wilkes, 22 July 1921 (as cited in Dagbovie, 2004)

The Business Wellbeing Coach or Unity of Hexagons offers coaching to fellow women colleagues who might be lucky enough to break the glass ceiling but not fortunate enough to break the invisible barriers in their minds for literature inclusion of ethnic minority women authors like myself who do not conform any political criteria of the fashionable agendas. I believe political neutrality allows women writers and visual artists from ethnic minority backgrounds to be more authentic and independent of oppressive practices outside political platforms. If I am offered a public space to exhibit my artwork and reach public audience without any oppressive political restriction, I will be able to reveal that, at last, I experience non-political literature/artistic inclusion in the UK. Otherwise, visual arts and literature events stay a commodity of the politically powerful class for their oppressive practice within the public gallery systems and literature festivals. I will be tapping into the human resources of the developing countries and see how I will contribute to their cultural developments through my literature and visual arts as a producer. I wonder whether or not I will face similar barriers I faced in the UK in the developing countries without sufficient public funding for literature and visual arts outlets. I shall find out the answers to my query sooner or later.

Academic curriculums and mental health

Many academic education systems discourage learning for the joy of learning. Alarmingly, academic students are more and more conditioned to produce their essays, thesis, dissertations and reports for the sake of passing their written exams without enjoying academic research. Academic students have no time left for reading and writing processes through stimulating reflection and critical thinking in order to digest academic concepts without being overwhelmed by the size of knowledge available for each discipline online and hardcopies in research libraries. The joy of learning for its own value lost its meaning when there is a strict deadline to meet for a lot of demanding research projects within very short intervals between each academic assignment over a two-semester time. Generally speaking, the majority of academic course curriculums from science to humanities is usually crammed with so many unrelated subjects which confuse many academic students. Students' brain is expected to switch on and off with a robotic mechanical process of writing. Moreover, some of the academic students are asked to sit for several written exams while they are trying to meet their deadlines for the submissions of three or four written assignments with the overstretched wordcount such as 10.000; 8.000 and 6.000 word count.

There is no time for a decent break, have a meal, get a goodnight sleep or to do shopping over the exam periods. Consequently, some of the academic students face physical and nervous breakdowns. According to the Institute for Public Policy Research (IPPR, 2017) a large number of students committed suicide in 2015. Between 2007 and 2015, the number of student suicides increased by 79 per cent in the UK. Some of my students couldn't get enough hours for one-to-one specialist mentoring support for overcoming the difficulties from mild depression to severe depression they've been experiencing alongside their study support during their academic studies. I've witnessed the deprivation of students' legal entitlement for proper access to one-to-one specialist mentoring support which destroyed not only students' physical and mental wellbeing but their academic performance at the same time. Some of my students faced discrimination within the academic establishments without sufficient provision to advocate their legal rights to learn wellbeing strategies provided by the trained specialist mentors but not by the lay persons or peer support groups only.

I strongly recommend that the academic staff should reassess the demanding academic course curriculum and readjust it in accordance with the average students' ability to cope so that students will complete their academic studies without reaching their breaking point. Academic students should be encouraged to learn for the sake of learning or the joy of acquiring new knowledge within the capacity of human mind. There is no need to overstretch their resources mentally, physically and financially. Business wellbeing coach offers alternative solutions to academic students on their academic studies without stigmatizing them or labelling for mental health difficulties they experience at some point of their lives. Everyone, regardless the strengths or weaknesses of their coping strategies under the harsh internal realities of academic life finds themselves helpless for a temporary period of time during their academic studies. If academic students don't receive instant support while they experience the early symptoms of anxiety, panic attack and mild depression, mental health problems will trap them for life and deprive them from fulfilling their personal and professional goals. Let's make learning easier and enjoyable for academic students but not harmfully stressful! That's my vision to achieve when I work with academic students as a specialist tutor/mentor/wellbeing coach.

Reflection on practical experience

I've been through the higher education system as a learner and educator since the late 1970s. I've learned a lot by doing continuous research on academic findings; critical analysis; evaluations of academic researchers; semi-academic writers and creative writing of non-academic writers. I appreciate theoretical learning; equally, I value learning from life itself through practical experience. I believe there is a vast amount of free resources in life which we all have an access to. Fellow human beings we meet daily are the source of human knowledge about themselves, animals and their environments. Sometimes, we are lucky to get to know many people because of the nature of our jobs as teachers, doctors, nurses and service providers. In some cases, people work in isolation without meeting anyone to have a deep discussion like sole traders. However, there is always enough time for us to explore life through different mediums such as taking a good walk in a countryside or in an urban setting. It is possible to learn new things through regular observations of our immediate environment. Human beings have got an ability to learn from any condition or environment on their own and in group settings. What we learn from our daily interactions with others outside school or academic environment by observing our natural environment, domestic and wild animals will get lost its importance if we don't record our learnings in the same way academic research students do.

We need to keep asking ourselves what type of recording process works for us. I use photography to remind me the new places I visited. It is a very enjoyable learning process to assess my own development when I am reflecting on my emotional intelligence and how it has been developing over the years from one photography trip to another one within different time frames. Years fly by me so rapidly. Sometimes I might even forget about the name of the places I visited or the people I met when I don't record their details. Some of the people I made connection with would stay within my network for life; some of them would get faded away with a lack of intention to keep in touch regularly on both sides. No matter, how short the connection last with each person I met over the course of my lifespan, there is always something I've gained from each human interaction. When I visit the same places twice or third times, there is always something to compare and contrast with besides finding surprising outcomes for the better or worst. I am constantly growing emotionally, intellectually and spiritually when I build up new memories through recording them via photography or writing about them in my books. Whenever I reflect on different stages of my personal evaluation process, I see the difference between the past time and current time as my insights being enriched by the visual, written and audio records of my experience with fellow human beings, animals and rapidly changing environment to give me a balanced view about who I am and who others are.

In each discipline, academic students are asked to keep a professional development journal to record their reflections on what they've learned, why they've learned and how they're planning to expand their learning for their future researches.

What is missing in a collective learning is the unrecorded process of our learning experience. Once academic students gain their first degree, they move on to the next level and take their second degree, for instance. Then, they get occupations or set up their own business as sole traders or choose business partnerships. Consequently, they stop recording what they learn from life, work or holiday trips. Without recording what we learn regularly, our brain unloads the experience of practical knowledge. Sometimes, our proactive learning is removed permanently from our long-term memory which causes us absence of reflective thinking.

Without sufficient reflective thinking, human beings do not make much progress as there is a loss of practical knowledge in the neurological pathways of our brain; that is why I highly recommend my students to keep up with recording their learning long after they have completed their academic studies. When I coach my students, I ask them to record their daily experiences such as what makes them happy, unhappy, fulfilled, being rewarded or being undervalued. I realize that the students who do their self-analysis and record their subjective findings about themselves are more reflective which makes it a lot easier for them to recognize their own needs, strengths, weaknesses and what they want to do with their lives. Coaching sessions become more meaningful by eliminating useless excuses of not knowing what we want from each coaching session or from our life.

In Jul 2017, I was contacted by a father of a medical student who failed from three written exams. The gentleman was very upset that his daughter might be asked to leave medicine. I comforted the distressed father over the phone and promised him to have an initial session with his daughter to identify how I could help her. When we had an initial session, I understood that medical student who was holding her first degree in science wasn't quite sure whether she wanted to work as a medical doctor or not. It was her second year in medicine and she had another three years to complete her studies providing she passed her exams. The situation the medical student was in, looked so complicated to me. She had only one month to grasp the revision technique covering the seven modules for the three written exams she was expected to sit. The medical student had a full-time summer job and didn't want to give up her full-time job whilst she needed to focus on her revision. It was so obvious that this young medical student didn't choose medicine because of a strong passion to become a medical doctor. She didn't fill up the paper I prepared for her to do self-analysis of her strengths and weaknesses before the coaching session took place. She was reluctant to complete her self-analysis during the initial session. There was a mental blockage which couldn't be resolved instantly. I knew that the young medical student lacked reflective thinking skills. If we had about ten sessions, there was a strong possibility that she was going to achieve what she really wanted to achieve in her academic life. Sadly, the medical student had never contacted me. I suspected that she dropped out of medicine realizing that she wasn't able to learn seven modules within less than a month time whilst holding a full-time job.

If only the young medical student had met me before she completed her first degree in science, she would have gained the analytical skills to identify what she wanted to get out of her second degree. More importantly, she would be able to make her plans to achieve her academic goals without stretching herself beyond her limits. Business Wellbeing Coach interacts with students in order to give them a chance to become reflective thinkers as they need enough time for reflection besides lateral thinking process for improvisation duration of an academic year. It is not possible for any student to become a competent achiever overnight. Learning is a slow process which needs to be spread over the extended period of time in order to digest what is learnt in theory and demonstrate knowledge in practice during the exam period. Learning requires undying patience and persistent practice in order to reach the core competence in any subject specialism area without giving up learning or relearning and renewing one's mental capacity to stretch its blockages. According to the best seller author, Malcolm Gladwell, mastery of any subject specialism requires 10,000 hours commitment as suggested in his book titled *Outliers* (2008).

> "The 10,000-hours rule says that if you look at any kind of cognitively complex field, from playing chess to being a neurosurgeon, we see this incredibly consistent pattern that you cannot be good at that unless you practice for 10,000 hours, which is roughly ten years, if you think about four hours a day."

Gladwell, 2008

I agree with Gladwell's finding based on his research study of the successful individuals. When we look at any successful person's life story, there is hard evidence to justify why they are outstanding not only in terms of their achievement which is the outcome but also in terms of their commitment and the amount of time they spent while they have been refining their skills through practice which is the input. If one has to formulate outstanding success, my suggested formula should be as follows:

Daily Input + Monthly Input + Yearly Input = 1st Achievement Outcome

If we double the amount of yearly input within six months by increasing 4 hours daily practice to 8 hours a day, the mastery of competence could be achieved within 5 years in each subject specialist area such as playing a piano; writing a book; accomplishing master pieces in visual arts and becoming a neuroscientist. There is no shortcut when it comes to the topic of mastery of the skills, abilities and professional competence. Smart people got smart answers to the question of their success which usually manifest their determination for wanting to achieve whatever they wanted to achieve with a single-minded approach to persistent practice beyond human limitations which include time, energy and resources.

We don't possess anything except our memories

When I looked at the lives of the rich and the poor what I realized was that there was one mutual condition. Neither the rich nor the poor possess anything except their memories of wealth or destitute when they face their mortality. Everyone becomes equal once they complete their life journey regardless they had a prosperous life style or endured a lack of possessions such as wealth, shelter, cloth, status, fame or legend of any kind.

The problem the whole humanity has been facing for centuries is that not being able to accept our mortality as the only ultimate reality we are going to come to terms with. Because of the inability to accept our unescapable destiny as mortal beings, the majority of us keep on striving for more and more possessions in life when there is no need for more than enough in some cases. I met very wealthy property investors feeling very pride of their possessions when they were disclosing the size of their property portfolio in public. One of the property investors claimed that he possesses 100 buy-to-let properties. I thought the number of the properties was more than enough to occupy oneself with until I heard another property investor disclosing his 500 buy-to-let properties. I questioned myself what motivated the middle-aged property investors to possess

100 or 500 properties. I don't think properties made them all happy. They didn't look they were content with what they had already possessed as they were after expanding their wealth further. I made a bit of calculation with their left-over years; the amount of the wealth they acquired and what they would do with it assuming they spent a million pound a year. Supposing they spent a million pound annually with the most luxurious life style; supposing they survived the average life span of 71, they wouldn't possibly run out of their wealth. What is the point of accumulating some more if they are unable to consume their wealth before passing away? The strange thing about these obsessive individuals with wealth is that they think everyone has got the same obsession to possess a property portfolio of 500 or more. I personally do not want to make my life complicated with the useless properties which might cause me inconvenience as there is a possibility of losing my inner peace. I dislike watching advertisements which keep on conditioning us that we would be better off if we had more possessions. Where is the hard evidence for that?

Even human relationship has been treated as some kind of possessions. Many people lost the importance of a genuine friendship without possessing them for life. Human relationships are turned into a power struggle of knowing who controls whom and for what financial gain. There isn't any freedom of equality in obsessive human relationships. An artificial friendship puts an enormous strain on our autonomy without enjoying a decent connection with its equal balance of respect and kindness for each other's rights to be ourselves. If we keep remembering that we do not possess anything except our memories, we'll be more fulfilled individuals without striving for more and more possessions. Business Wellbeing Coach works on human weaknesses for acquiring more possessions without knowing where to stop. Clients are encouraged to see the wealth of the meaningful memories and keep on building up their best memories before it might be too late to do so if our life is cut short by unpredictable circumstances such as incurable diseases or tragic traffic accidents. Sadly enough, I have met a lot of unhappy people striving for more and more possessions during their younger years; the majority of them ended up losing the quality of life when they were physically deteriorated and not being able to enjoy a simple food before passing away. When there is a time for some of us to enjoy what we already possess such as ability to walk, eat, breath, sleep without much difficulty, we need to make the most of our life without losing our perspective for what is essential what is not to achieve the optimum wellbeing.

Ransomware hackers corrupt their intelligence

Some of my students have been experiencing financial hardship. Their laptops were damaged and they didn't have money to replace their broken laptops. Some of them didn't even have their own laptops. Laptop is an essential device for academic students to be successful in their academic studies. Without owning their own laptop, academic students can't make much progress in acquiring academic research skills such as active reading strategy and critical analysis of literature. When I realized some of my students' extreme poverty without having their own laptops for face-to-face tutorials, I felt it was impossible for them to gain research skills for reading up-to-date academic journals online. Consequently, I decided to buy a notepad so that I could take the notepad to the face-to-face sessions each time I met my students in a public space. I also bought Microsoft office software to go with the hardware, which cost me an additional expense. However, it resolved the shortage of the hardware some of my students experiencing during the academic year 2015 and 2016. Then, my notepad was hacked. I lost the PDF file reader. I decided to download the free PDF file reader online. The free PDF file reader turned out to be the ransomware; the hackers locked out my notepad and demanded a ransom in return for access. The IT person who looks after my electronic devices couldn't come around to remove the ransomware which prevented me from using the notepad for my teaching practice that caused me a lot of inconvenience for the whole year. Just recently, I've checked my notepad to figure out how I could remove the ransomware from my notepad. I did a bit of research online. I've found Avast Free Antivirus software. I've installed the software on my notepad. The free antivirus didn't remove the ransomware. Avast Free Antivirus software supplier demanded subscription fee with 1 year, 2 years and 3 years options instead. I've come to the conclusion that Avast Free Antivirus software must be another ransomware. I am annoyed with the unscrupulous hackers who choose an unethical way of making money for a living. The difference between sex workers and ransomware hackers is that the sex workers prostitute their bodies, the ransomware hackers prostitute their intelligence which could have been used to make a living from ethical channels.

I remember watching a strange interview on Channel 4 News program that was produced by ITN and has been around since 1982 in the UK. The political correspondent, Cathy Newman was interviewing a woman prostitute who claimed that there was nothing wrong to work in sex industry as it was her choice. The sex worker was justifying the corrupted way of making a living out of prostitution. I was shocked by the presenter, Cathy Newman's interaction with a dissolute woman. I couldn't help being irritated by the fact that the Channel 4 News Staff had chosen the useless topic which wasn't in the best interest of the general public who pay TV license in the UK. There is a strong probability that the interview could confuse youngsters about what is ethical and what isn't after being manipulated by the prostitute's justification of her depraved life style. Furthermore, the arrogant prostitute's irrational justification could only have a bad impact on youngsters if the ill-fated person is taken like a role model by some of the blameless teenagers. There are a lot of destitute women in the UK and some of them do refuse to prostitute themselves for a living when they face starvation. The political correspondent, Newman could be more helpful if she was able to provide a platform for the unadulterated poor women with ethical preference to avoid corruption in every aspect of their lives that should be actively encouraged but not the other way around. When there is news about offshore investment practice amongst well-known public figures, the media representatives use a very offensive language to criticize the wrong doing of certain individuals. Unfortunately, the same criticism didn't apply to the prostitute who is justifying the immoral way of earning a living shamelessly in public.

The Business Wellbeing Coach provides a remedy for the media staff who lacks of inspiration on how to increase ethical standards of the media coverages. I wonder whether or not there is an Ethical Standard Committee to monitor the contents of Channel 4 News. If there is an Ethical Standard Committee for media profession, the following question needs to be answered.

> *"Why doesn't the Ethical Standard Committee function within the framework of Code of Ethics any public service provider is expected to comply with?"*

Within the public education system from primary school level to university level, none of the educators is allowed to promote prostitution implicitly or explicitly as civil servants. Otherwise, their inappropriate comment will be taken as a serious offence for persecution or dismissal. Similarly, Channel 4 News Team has got a responsibility to leave out justification of prostitution and damaging pornography from their news' contents which are still considered improper behavior for the majority of the families with teenage children in the UK or abroad.

All types of extremism are harmful!

Moderation is good for everything in life without exploiting our human capacity to function properly. When we think about our eating habits or our spending power for daily expenses; occasional treats for ourselves or others, we will be better off without stretching our financial resources beyond our means. There is no need to go into bad debts. Instead, we ought to learn how to budget and manage our living cost within the limitation of our financial resources. Individuals and organizations must have a financial plan which should be realistic in terms of our survival needs within our budget. If our needs cannot be met through our financial resources, we will be in trouble not only financially but physically and emotionally. Stretching our financial resources would bring stress which causes internal toxic in our body. Our mind is affected by negative thinking process as each negative thought destroys the balance of our body, mind and spirit gradually.

I met academic students who are unaware of budgeting skills. They found themselves out of pocket at the end of each month because they spent their money on luxurious expenses but not essentials such as buying an expensive present for a child without realizing that a child hasn't got any mental capacity to appreciate the most expensive present. A small inexpensive present without destroying someone's budget should be sufficient enough for a child to be happy with. There should be enough money left in our pocket to cover the daily expenses for the cost of travel and food. I realize that not only young adults lack the ability of budgeting but also adults with dependents. In my ESOL class in 2003, I met a young married woman with her two teenage children. When her husband became obsessed with purchasing the most expensive cars which led him into bad debt threatening their survival, she had to leave her husband. The young mother had no choice but to bring up her children on her own working very hard including at weekends and during summer time without taking any time off. Her health gradually declined; she lost her mobility and suffered from chronic depression. It was a tragic family separation due to the thoughtless husband's obsession with the luxury goods to feed his ego for showing off.

If we look at some countries with poverty on the rise amongst young generations despite their rich natural resources like petrol, it is easy to pinpoint the problem. Most of the time, poverty is caused as a result of a lack of financial management skills but not a lack of money. Let's have a look at Saudi Arabia as the world's leading oil exporter with the capacity of the second largest producer. Logical thinking assumes nobody would suffer from financial crises in Saudi Arabia. The average citizens should be able to lead a modest lifestyle without going hungry. Unfortunately, this is not the case! When I watched the news on media, I was surprised to hear that young Saudi Arabians with the 2nd degrees are unemployed; they don't know how they are going to survive. Yet, Saudi Arabia employs over 7 million foreign nationalities. What is going wrong with their system? The majority of the population in Saudi Arabia is Muslim. The religion imposes on Muslim population not to fall into an extravagance trap of unlimited spending habits regardless they possess an excessive amount of wealth. The rich citizens live in isolation from the less fortunate class who are struggling to survive. The distribution of wealth is not balanced.

The same financial discrimination applies to European countries like Italy with **$1.81 trillion** economy which is classified as the world's ninth GDP rank (Investopedia, 2017). During my research trip to Venice in 2015, I met an elderly disabled beggar woman whose body bended that looked painful to me when I visualized myself in that uncomfortable position for a long time. She was wearing a black long dress and covering her hair with a black scarf. Her face and body couldn't be seen. The heat was unbearable. I couldn't help noticing the small paper tea container she was holding without any coin in it. The tourists were ignoring her tragedy. I put 1 Euro into her container and walked down to see the world's most glamorous art exhibitions in Venice Biennial. After spending hours seeing the most expensive art displays, I came to the same point where I met the poor Italian old beggar woman who was there in the early morning. She was still bending in the same uncomfortable position with the empty paper container. It was very upsetting to witness the beggar woman's tragedy. I felt sorry for the underprivileged disabled elderly woman. I didn't think that she deserved to be turned into a beggar woman on the street where there were plenty luxurious shops, art galleries and wealthy merchants' splendid houses. While the wealthy class of the nation were enjoying the highest standard, the little disabled elderly woman was left abandoned to starve without anyone noticing her tragic existence. I took a photo of the Italian beggar woman bending next to the posh gallery advertisement. Each time I look at the photo of the beggar woman taken on my European trip, 2015, I see the juxtaposition between the two-extremist human existence; one is an immense luxury of the wealthy class and the other one is an extreme deprivation of the dying beggar woman in Venice Biennale. Who is responsible for the misery of an old Italian woman? Could it be individuals' responsibility or local authorities? Are we all responsible for her destitute since we cannot bear to witness such a human suffering on the street or on the news without having any power to improve her life circumstances?

I visited South of France in 2015 as part of my photography research trip. I was in Nice staying in a clean hotel overlooking the pleasant scenery. There was an elderly French homeless woman sitting on the street bench having all her belongings inside the several bags around her under the strong heat. Whenever I left the hotel for sightseeing she was there in the same place. When I came back to hotel late evening she was still there. It was like time stopped for the poor French woman. Without leaving her small world which could be taken up by another beggar, I assumed she spent days and nights at the same spot during the hot summer. I wonder how she fed and washed herself. I couldn't help feeling distressed on my holiday worrying about the old French woman living outside without leaving the street bench for the fear of losing it. I asked myself what happens to her during the winter time. Obviously, she couldn't sit on the same bench in the open air when it rained or snowed; how many years she has been living on the street like that; how about the local authorities? Were the local authorities unable to accommodate her in a social home for elderly people? Who was responsible to comfort the homeless French woman in her undignified circumstances in a relevantly rich country which is recorded as the seventh largest economies with a nominal GDP of **$2.42 trillion** (Investopedia, 2017).

I had a BA student doing her degree in social science in 2016. She explored the gender inequality in her assignment. During her research project, I discovered the outcast widows in India.

I watched the documentary film titled *The Invisible Women: Outcast Widows in India (2015)* which was as distressing as seeing the realities of the female beggars within their impoverished life struggle in the big cities such as London, Venice and Nice. If the politicians felt responsibility to improve the most vulnerable underclass people without ignoring their distressful circumstances, things could have improved for the poor and the needy ages ago. What would have happened if the powerful politicians had slept on the street for a month experiencing homelessness with their homeless fellow human beings? Would the politicians gain an insight into homelessness? Would they understand what the homeless people go through in their lives on the street? Would the exercise help the politicians develop compassion towards the homeless population without anywhere to sleep? Who knows it might have done the trick to open the politicians' spiritual eye!

The sad story of a British classical pianist, Anne Naysmith couldn't be foreseen for some middle-class British in the 20th century. Anne Naysmith (1937 – 2015) was born in Essex and brought up in a comfortable family to start with. Anne studied at the Royal Academy of Music in London. At the age of 18, she rented a room in Chiswick and worked as a music teacher at a convent school in Berkshire and at Trinity College of Music in London. At the age of 25, Anne played Bach and Beethoven at Leighton House in London. In 1967 Anne's mother hired the Wigmore Hall in London for her to perform as a pianist. By the early 70s, Miss Naysmith had given up teaching. Strangely enough, nobody knows the reason why Anne gave up teaching; I presume that Anne was unfairly dismissed from her teaching position which is always the case for unmarried female school teachers or single female public servants as a matter of unfair practice. Anne was forced to leave her rented accommodation due to the fact that she couldn't afford to pay the rent after being unfairly dismissed from her teaching post. Since then, Anne lived in her car for 26 years until 2002. According to Guardian newspaper (2015), Anne Naysmith took a shelter in a school doorway most nights after night classes finished and would be left before school began next day during the last ten years of her life. When Anne was killed by a lorry at the age 78 in London, she already completed 38 years of her life sentence on the street in absolute misery. Some arrogant individuals made sarcastic comments about Anne's life suggesting that it was her choice to live on the street. I doubt if it was her own choice. I am sure that Anne wouldn't reject the idea of being rehoused by social services when she was no longer able to keep up with rent payment. Anne refused the patronising attitude of the middle class. The decent English woman was desperate for charitable compassion to be rehoused for free accommodation. I still can't understand how the devoted Christian woman at an old age was left unprotected to sleep rough in the cold and rainy days. There is no excuse to cover up the human tragedy with pompous words as follows:

> *"One day many years ago I heard her singing like an angel in the street. It was obvious she was a talented musician. Sometimes I felt sorry for her, but often I reflected that, with that fierce pride of hers, she probably never felt sorry for herself."*

Robert Fish, 2015

> *"Not a nice way to go but … she lived her life exactly the way she chose – and for that alone … round of applause!"*

Stuart Kerr, 2015

Be realistic please! Don't humiliate Anne Naysmith, at least, after what she had gone through in life. The local authorities had a capacity and political power to provide a free shelter for Anne when she was no longer able to keep up with her rent payment for private accommodation. The useless words recorded in the newspapers didn't provide any remedy for Anne's tragedy when she was alive. The well-presented media coverage could have transformed Anne's misery into a decent living condition during her life time. Disappointedly enough, the British news channels like Channel 4 News or the political correspondent, Cathy Newman wasn't particularly interested in bringing up tragic life events of the innocent sufferers like Anne Naysmith who died poor, homeless and socially excluded but never compromised from her moral dignity without prostituting herself that should be rewarded. God bless Anne Naysmith's spirit in abundance where her spirits resides now! Let's stop talking irrationally and start doing something beneficial for all the vulnerable elderly population aging on the streets of the big cities all over the world before rushing them to heaven in worst conditions. The world resources are sufficient enough to cater the poor and the needy without stretching the middle-class population's resources especially in the UK with a **$2.5 trillion** GDP which is categorized as the world's fifth largest economy despite its Brexit referendum result (Investopedia, 2017).

Equality Act 2010 has been challenged!

I am registered with the Disabled Students' Allowance Quality Assurance Group (DSA-QAG) which is a database system for specialist tutors/mentors to be contacted by disabled students themselves who are diagnosed as dyslexic and eligible for DSA-funded support when they want to choose their independent providers. The Non-Medical Helper Providers (NMH): Quality Assurance Framework identifies the procedure as follows

> *Any student who undergoes a study needs assessment from 28 April 2016 and requires NMH support, the provider must be selected from the DSA-QAG NMH register. All NMH providers on the register will need to conform to this quality assurance framework.*
>
> Transitional arrangements, p.8

On 04 Dec 2017, I experienced rather strange bullying and harassment tactic of the two different supply teaching agencies A and B. I was contacted by the administrator of the supply teaching agency A offering me two assignments as a specialist tutor. The students were assigned to me without completing the registration process with the agency in full. I was asked to take an irritating test which had no preparatory reading for multiple choice questions; some test questions were also formed wrongly. I was asked to provide my qualifications, DBS, professional indemnity insurance, my NIN and bank details. I provided everything assuming that the supply teaching agency A was safe as the agency A was registered with the DSA-QAG and I met her at the first DSA-QAG meeting in London. I was pressurized to contact two dyslexic students immediately and arranged the initial meetings with them at once. I was quite apprehensive about being rushed into an action without thinking much about what would follow next. I met the dyslexic students at different locations on 20th Dec and 21st Dec 2017. After meeting the students and committing myself to their support tuition arrangements, I received an absurd contract with 6 pages which restricts my employment statuary rights altogether. It occurred to me that the supply teaching agencies A and B might be part of a sham operation as part of conspiracy to get me out of my niche area of specialist teaching & mentoring dyslexic adults in HE/FE. My competitors demanded me to work for them without any employee benefits. I suspected that they were trying to trap me. If I was contracted to them with an absurd contract which imposes a legal binding on me, they would place themselves in a powerful position to exploit me as they please like human traffickers. I am a sole trader. Why did supply teaching agencies A and B ask me to work for them? Their intention was to ruin my professional life as it revealed to me gradually. Realizing their unethical purpose, I declined to sign the contract. They didn't pay me for the two support sessions I provided for the students despite the fact that I used my own resources such as cartridge, paper, phone calls and I paid travel fare to meet the students in public places. My two days were taken up by face-to-face meetings with the dyslexic students. The arrogant supply teaching agencies A and B did not apologize to me for their unprofessional conduct.

I immediately sent text messages to the students and let them know that I was no longer working for the supply teaching agencies A and B. One of the students contacted me and asked me what to do. I referred him back to the supply teaching agency A to ask for my replacement. When the agency B could not replace me instantly, the distressed student called me again and asked me whether I could support him instead as he already wasted 2 months and he had 3 written assignments to complete with very tight deadline. I could not see any harm to offer my service to rescue him from the stressful situation he was going through after all I was a registered provider myself with the professional indemnity insurance and I am on the DSA-QAG database as a NMH. The adult dyslexic student and I decided to meet the 2nd time on the date we agreed to meet on the initial meeting. We spent 3 hours in a public library; I suggested the student to make a request for a change of supplier which is the procedure he should follow as it was written in his DSA entitlement letter. He emailed his request to the Student Loan Company (SLC) and received an instance response to his request on the same day without any delay. It usually takes five working days for SLC administrators to reply to students' enquiries. The SLC advisor suggested the distressed student to contact the supply teaching agency B instead of dealing with his request for a change of supplier. The SLC advisor also forwarded the student's request for a change of supplier email to the supply teaching agencies A and B without seeking the dyslexic student's consent for that. The SLC advisor breached the Code of Confidentiality in relation to disabled students' rights. The SLC advisor discriminated the disabled student. Moreover, the advisor discriminated me as a NMH who is registered with DSA-QAG and eligible to support the DSA-funded student when there is a demand for it, especially the disabled student approached me directly.

The dyslexic student did not want to go back to supply teaching agency B who abused his consumer statuary rights in the first place for not being able to provide him a support tutor within the reasonable time. There was no point in pressurizing the disabled student to do something which was not acceptable. I offered the adult dyslexic student my service as an advocate to resolve the issues he was experiencing on his behalf as he didn't have any time or enough knowledge what to do. I prepared the second request email for a change of supplier and emailed it to the same SLC advisor who sounded like having a connection with the unprofessional supply teaching agencies A and B while she was acting as a gatekeeper and preventing me from supplying what the disabled student demanded which should be considered a fair competition that had occurred beyond my deliberate intention. The SLC advisor favored the supply teaching agencies A and B who breached the Code of Conduct by getting each other involved which the disabled student wasn't made aware of. I was asked to register with the supply teaching agency A. However, I was asked to work for the supply teaching agency B which is not acceptable as it is written in the Non-Medical Helper Providers: Quality Assurance Framework below:

> The NMH provider will be audited on a regular 12monthly interval depending on the size and range of services offered by the provider. NMH support cannot be contracted out to a third party. If the provider does not have the capacity to deliver the required support they should notify SFE so that another provider can be selected.
>
> The Principle Objective, p. 8

The amount of paperwork and emails I received from the supply teaching agencies A and B were beyond any NMH's expectation. When I searched for the supply teaching agency B on the DSA-QAG database register, I noticed that the agency appeared on the same page where my registration appears as if the provider was positioning himself with me. However, he didn't have either company registration number or any indication for how long his business has been around. I discovered that the supply teaching agency B which was assigned to the disabled students as their provider by the SLC administrator did not have a capacity to employ me as his employee. That must be the reason he was using the supply teaching agency A to register me in order to work for him as the provider of the supply teaching agency B. Things became too complicated for me to accept. I understood that he was using me in order to enter the DSA-QAG database registration. The two supply teaching agencies A and B exploited my good intention to trust them unconditionally without making enquiries about their trading history. The DSA-QAG administrator registered the supply teaching agency B which wasn't registered with HMRC. I still cannot comprehend how that happened. The SLC administrators allowed these peculiar supply teaching agencies A and B's unethical operation as the SLC advisor refused the dyslexic student's request for a change of supplier and referred him back on to supply teaching agency B.

I paid audit fee to register with the DSA-QAG database and I complied with all the tedious administrative procedure of reading official documents on a regular basis. I agreed with the terms and conditions in order to appear on their database as a NMH provider. What was the use of being registered with the DSA-QAG database, if I am not treated as fairly as other providers such as the supply teaching agency B whose company registration doesn't appear on the DSA-QAG registration. How could the need assessor get another quote from another supply teaching agency while the disabled student was allocated to me by the supply teaching agency A and B who were going to trap me if I didn't investigate their breach of Code of Conduct? The SLC advisor provoked the supply teaching agencies A and B against me by emailing them the disabled student's request for a change of supplier. I received abusive emails from the supply teaching agencies A and B accusing me of stealing their DSA-funded student whose legal right was originally abused by them. I realized that supply teaching agency B was going to exploit me for his advantage in conjunction with the supply teaching agency A with a 6-page contract acting like human traffickers. In the contract, it was recorded that I have to pay the agency A, £50 for lateness and £60 for cancellation of the assignment whilst the agency A, doesn't pay my NI, pension and holiday entitlement. The confusing articles of the employment contract are quoted below:

> **5.7**. *Should the Independent Contractor arrive late or fail to attend the assignment without a reasonable, valid and acceptable explanation, for which reason the assignment is wholly or partially frustrated and/or cancelled, and/or due to which Agency A is subjected to claim reduced income, the Independent Contractor shall be liable for the payment of a **£50.00** lateness fee as well as full fee recovery to the Company for the incurred loss, whichever is greater*

> **15.6** *If the Independent Contractor curtails or cancels an assignment or series of previously agreed assignments without following the termination procedure stipulated in the Contract and/or without a valid and acceptable reason*, they will be liable for payment of a **£60** cancellation fee per assignment and/or payment and recovery of incurred loss of business, whichever is greater. This shall also affect any future booking or student referral.*

One of my returning students contacted me 2 months ago and asked me to provide her support. I gave her my details to request from her need assessor to assign me as her NMH. The need assessor did not include me on her recommendation as her NMH. My student contacted the SLC advisor and explained that she wanted to have me back as her NMH. It was the second time the SLC advisor rejected my former student's request and didn't reply to my enquiry on what grounds he rejected me as a NMH during the selection procedure. It was clear to me that the DSA-QAG database register has not been set up for the SLC administrators to treat suppliers on their database equally. Far from receiving an equal treatment, the SLC team favors the corporate type suppliers but discriminate independent suppliers like myself. The SLC and the DSA-QAG are turned into a network mechanism which create lock-ins. With strategic lock-in, users become dependent on selected suppliers recommended by need assessors or disability teams. Consequently, disabled students are unable to switch to another supplier without being bullied and threatened with the withdrawal of their Disabled Student Allowances. When disabled students are doing their degrees in HE/FE, they get into a large amount of debt to pay their tuition fees; they deserve to be treated with respect and courtesy. Adult dyslexic students in HE/FE lost their autonomy within the obscure system created by the SLC. The intimidation disabled students face during their academic studies is not justifiable. Some need assessors receive a very high fee for assessing DSA-funded dyslexic students' need within the 2-hr session in the expense of neglecting students' statuary rights for selecting their own providers from the DSA-QAG database. I presume that some need assessors get a commission from the corporate type supply teaching agencies at the same time. Otherwise, they would have selected me as a registered independent NMH at least occasionally. Since I registered with DSA-QAG in 2016, I did not get any DSA-funded dyslexic student's referral directly from the SLC. I have been facing systematic discrimination coming from different sources such as need assessors, SLC administrators, disability advisors and a hostile senior librarian who worked in one of the universities in London while I was working as a NMH.

Independent providers like myself registered with the DSA-QAG are treated like unsolicited providers but not reliable professions whose input should be appreciated by academic staff in HE/FE. I understand that attending network events only helps the large and medium suppliers to target the independent suppliers with less visibility and get them out of the system as soon as their contribution is recognized by DSA-funded students. Market share is divided between the politically likeminded corporate supply teaching agencies only. I am not sure whether I will be able to attend DSA-QAG meeting in London in 2018. According to the Statistician, Rebecca Mantle (National Statistic, 2017), the number of the registered disabled undergraduate and postgraduate students in the UK was 279,115 (2016/2017). I had a zero DSA-funded student referred on to me by the SLC administrators out of 279,115 registered disabled students in the UK since my DSA-QAG registration in 2016.

I hope the audit fee I have already paid for the DSA-QAG in 2018 should be refunded. It will be unfair to be expected to pay the audit fee when I didn't receive my market share out of the registered 279,115 disabled student population last year. Neither need assessors nor disability teams would prepare to work for nothing. However, I am prepared to offer my skills for a job-share with disability provision if they are willing to share their earning capacity with me. It is necessary for all the administrators who work within disability provision to familiarize themselves with the Article 5 – Equality and Non-Discrimination as part of Convention on the Rights of Persons with Disabilities (2006) given below:

> *1. States Parties recognize that all persons are equal before and under the law and are entitled without any discrimination to the equal protection and equal benefit of the law.*
>
> *2. States Parties shall prohibit all discrimination on the basis of disability and guarantee to persons with disabilities equal and effective legal protection against discrimination on all grounds.*
>
> *3. In order to promote equality and eliminate discrimination, States Parties shall take all appropriate steps to ensure that reasonable accommodation is provided.*
>
> https://www.un.org/development/desa/disabilities/convention-on-the-rights-of-persons-with-disabilities/article-5-equality-and-non-discrimination.html [Accessed on 10 Jan 2018]

The dyslexic students attended their initial meeting with me on 20th Dec 2017 and 21st Dec 2017 didn't have an access to their NMH support while I was writing this article on 23rd Apr 2018. The disabled students' demand for a NMH support hasn't been supplied by the corporate supply teaching agencies A and B or any other corporate supply teaching agency so far. The students' requests for a change of supplier wasn't handled fairly by the SLC administrator; the disabled students completely disillusioned with the complexities caused to them by the SLC administrators during the last 5 months. There isn't anyone to deal with the complaints either. I have reached the conclusion that the disability provision didn't work in the best interest of disabled students since Dec 2017. It only worked in the best interest of the SLC administrative staff as they used a delaying tactic to change disabled students' mind by encouraging them to give up their legal entitlements for the DSA-funded support altogether. Damian Hinds MP was appointed as Secretary of State for Education on 8 January 2018. Let's hope that the new Secretary of State for Education will be able to resolve the issues created under Justine Greening's leadership. Otherwise, disabled students' suffering will continue alongside independent NMHs without fair treatment.

What is your focal point today?

I had a very demanding day yesterday. I needed to reply to the arrogant person's justification of discrimination within education system. Remembering all the negative experiences I had gone through made me upset. I had already missed the deadline for the submission of my forthcoming book. I had to extent my submission date longer than 2 and a ½ months because of the unethical supply teaching agencies' interference with my professional life. I wasted my precious time while I was corresponding with dysfunctional administrators. Time is money in any business as it is the most precious commodity. Our life is geared towards meeting non-stop deadlines. To destruct anyone's life with all the complications and conspiracies is not right at all. I have learnt my lesson from the bad experience with a high price which disrupted my daily routine. I went to bed at 2:30 am in the morning. I had a restless sleep as I was still suffering from the consequences of meeting the unprofessional people; it was very irritating to remember how I was exploited by them. Reflecting on the disastrous outcomes of the unpleasant experience with unethical competitors for 50 days had a negative effect on my wellbeing emotionally and financially.

I would have been wiser if I refused the business offer in the first place. How could I know what I was going to experience? Sometimes, we are unable to predict the consequences of any negative business transaction. It is always necessary to get out of the distressful situation as quickly as possible to avoid more damages on our health and business.

Today is Saturday. I got up at 10:00 am. I kept positive by focusing on my future plans such as how I could turn the bad experience into a creative outcome for my writing career. All of a sudden, the negative aspect of the bad experience lessened its damaging stress factor. I started singing aloud as though I was not going through the distressful period of my life with all the inconvenience caused to me by the unethical people. When I reached the end of day, I was feeling already elevated with the positive energy. I had a pleasant evening with a homemade dinner. I felt grateful to my Creator once more that He blessed me with an ability to see the positive things happening in my life even during the time when I was facing adversity. I told myself if I focused on the bad things only, I wouldn't be able to enjoy my dinner fully. I am very lucky that I don't stay in a negative state of mind for a long time. I acquired the skill of switching from negativity to positivity within a short time. I visualize the meaningful days ahead of me, the most beautiful places which I have not been before and the people with moral integrity whom I haven't met yet.

On a daily basis, I need to find one positive thing to finish my day with. It is like working on your profit and loss account daily. What did you gain throughout a day? What was the highlight of your day? What did you learn from your human experience of being alive? Is there any possibility to reach the equilibrium state of mind before going to sleep over your bad day? What is the most important thing in your life? Is your focal point still animated by your vision? Are you focusing on what makes your life more meaningful? When I meditate I sense the removal of my negativity from my metabolism so that it'll get a lot easier for me to fall asleep.

Looking at the photos from my photography trips takes me back to the positive mood I was in during the happy times of my life. Then, I start realizing that time is relative. All the good memories and bad ones will be in our personal history in a few years' time. There is no guarantee in our life for how long we will be around. When time is too precious to lose, the best practice is to use it wisely without wasting. If I treat time like water from the water container when there is no rain, the water needs to last longer. I make all the effort to benefit every single minute of what I have left with for the rest of my life. I was doing research on 'Experiential Marketing' today in the morning, the doorbell rang. I wasn't expecting any guest or a delivery by post. I didn't answer the door. I couldn't afford to waste more time as I have already wasted my 50 days and I am far behind my time schedule for my deadline. I thought life is like that. There is not much to extend longer than the average life span; why bother losing the most precious commodity for nothing. I didn't feel guilty for not answering the doorbell. I thought if it was an important call, I would have notified it beforehand. Our mortality is on its way to ring the doorbell of our life and we'll be asked to leave everything, including the most important projects we have committed ourselves to complete, the most beautiful places we planned to visit and the most precious artefact we wanted to treat ourselves with. When the time comes for us to leave this life, there won't be any time for us to spend. Everything will be over for our future plans. It's like sitting for a difficult exam. You read the question and start answering the question without realizing how quickly time passes. Then, the invigilator reminds you "stop writing; exam is over; I'll collect the exam papers shortly." Most of the time, students wish they had a bit more time to put their thoughts down in a more structured way or change a few sentences before handing their paper over the invigilator. There is no time to add or remove anything from the exam paper when the exam is over. Remember, there will be the last minute of our life sooner or later. Then, our internal clock will be stopped forever on this part of our life. Therefore, it is important not to answer each time the doorbell rings unexpectedly. Don't forget that you will never have a chance to complete what you aim to complete before you meet your mortality if you answer the unexpected doorbells all the time. Our life becomes more worthwhile with the precious things we select by our unique choices but also what we eliminate from our daily life such as a waste of time with anti-social people. A mortal writer needs to avoid all the clutter not only on her desk when she starts writing but all the unnecessary interference of external realities.

I would have been better off if I didn't respond to the calls the unethical business people made by stealing my precious time from me while I was planning to extend my limited life span with the things which meant a lot to me but not with the meaningless things such as conspiracies prepared by my aggressive competitors. We need to be selective in life. The more selective we are the happier and healthier we become. It is important for our wellbeing to know when to answer the doorbell and when to ignore it. If we can't make a decision what to do when the doorbell rings unexpectedly, there is a strong possibility that we'll lose our focal point in life which will cause the unsuccessful completion of our journeys without having had enough time to live for our ideals but being kept busy with non-stop conspiracies only. Time is too short to waste for meaningless vicious circle of bad experiences. We need to know how to push the unethical people out of our business life. Then, we become more efficient in terms of getting the balance right when we reflect on our profit and loss account on a daily basis. What I gained today was the learning point of my professional life as a writer. I appreciate how precious time has been for me and how I have lived my day for myself without letting anyone to distract me during the 24 hours life span. That's my victory! Business Wellbeing Coach encourages clients to build up their meaningful time management by gaining the skills how to allocate each working day not only to be successful but be happy and content with what we have left after eliminating all the clutters out of our life.

Robots with emotional intelligence!

When I met a robot Pepper on a cruise ship in 2017, I thought I met a very nice fellow passenger with human warmth. I spent quite a lot of time interacting with a human-like robot. Pepper gave me useful information using human expressions which are related to our emotions. I was fascinated by observing how the robot engaged her audience with her human like gestures. Pepper even asked us whether we would like to have our photos taken with her. Then, she gave her elegant poses from different angles which made us all laugh. Children started touching her hands. I put my arm over her shoulder whilst my photo was taken with her. There was a very good bond one might get with pets or special people who might have empathic sensitivity to attract our fascination.

Today, I read about experiential marketing and how it works for the 21st century consumers while conventional marketing strategies assume us less than what we are by conditioning us to become robots without any emotional intelligence unlike Pepper as she doesn't fit into the classification of an ordinary robot. I recognize Pepper as an exceptional robot who was transformed into a human being by a clever robot designer.

According to the estimated figures, 30 years ago an average American was exposed to 560 daily advertisements, today, the average consumer is exposed to 3,000 to 4,000 marketing messages (Max Lenderman, 2006). Media jungle and large corporations with huge marketing budget controls consumers to act certain way as they want us to shop without thinking about what we buy and why we buy on impulse. Aggressive selling strategies reduce consumers' autonomy. We are treated like a mass product of the same factory produced by the same machinery without human emotions as if we are all mass-produced robots without a particular preference for individualized service. The conventional selling strategies do not work for the people who do not conform the serialization of consumerism mania.

Even in teaching industry, teaching any discipline to different students with various learning preferences and aptitudes, cannot be successful without using differentiation strategy by treating each student as a unique individual but not part of the mass products of this century ready to receive data input. Unfortunately, students are treated like consumers without human emotions during conventional classroom teaching from primary school level to university degree level. Teachers are trained to get the same results from the old teaching methods. Students' performance is measured by how much factual information he/she keeps in their short-term memory rather than how they make use of factual information within different environments for creative solutions.

University students are treated like unintelligent consumers, who are exposed to the conditioning advertisement packages of traditional commercialism. They get bored with the subjects they study and lose their interest in their subject specialism areas gradually. Some of them, even become skeptical about the purpose of their studies whilst they start questioning themselves whether they will be better off switching to another subject once history becomes a distressing phenomenon; anthropology loses its essence when students exposed to its origin through colonialism; architecture design becomes conventional design; legal studies turns into a problem without solution; computing becomes a machine language; medicine becomes more factual than practice with limited resources and so on.

What needs to be considered, which is neglected for a long time in any business interaction is personalized one-to-one approach to our needs as a consumer, a student, an employee, a client, a friend, a parent, a sibling, a neighbor and a citizen. Providers need to treat users as individuals with specific variables which cannot be generalized as 'one method fit for all mentality' in each industry from teaching, marketing, hospitality, medicine, entertainment, music, media, literature, visual arts, catering and sport. What needs to be explored in each industry is that how to turn service or product delivery into a unique customer experience without turning it into banality. The more humanized the customer relation gets with personalized products or services, the more satisfied the outcomes will be with specific human values e.g. appreciation and happiness as a result of being valued through social inclusion which will eradicate the bad feelings of mistreatments such as being left out, undervalued and overlooked within any anti-social business transaction. What is the use of making money out of belittling your client, student or employee? There is no value attached to any profit made out of destroying confidence of your students, clients, employees or customers. If providers lose their human values, any service or product will be turned into a demoralizing tool for the users to experience. The majority of businesses go into bankruptcy not because a lack of skills in terms of technical competence but a lack of human connection with their consumers.

I lost many of my friends when they started treating me as their rival competitor in a ruthless employment environment. I lost confidence in some of my old friends. I would have preferred to have friendship without being exposed to the aggressive consumerism mania. I would have loved to be treated as a human being without being controlled or told what political party I should vote, how I should live, whom I should be in touch with and where I should live. Some of my old friends treated me like I was possessed by them. Instead of losing my human integrity, I decided to end my friendship with them as I do not fit into the cycle of conformist people who want to have the same preferences. I look for a genuine human quality in friendship. I dislike being treated like a machine by being pushed or pulled to the direction I have no intention to be drifted when I really want to focus on my focal point which is completely different than my friends, colleagues, family members, relatives and neighbors. The Business Wellbeing Coach stays in tune with clients' agenda for their own choices what they want from each human relationship including friendship but not being pressurized to fulfil others' expectations.

Market Share

I have recently discovered an expression which appears as strategic disturbance. According to Stacey (1993), strategy in a business term is all about handling disturbance. Handling disturbance demands taking control of the situation.

> *"The starting point is not the mission, and certainly not detailed long term objectives, but the appropriate style of control."*
>
> Stacey (1993) as cited in Thompson & Martin, 2010, p.51

In the book titled *Strategic Management, Awareness & Change,* John Thompson and Frank Martin (2010) suggest that disturbances can come from anywhere and everywhere such as loss of customers, change of regulations, taxation and appearance of new competitors. When disturbance occurs, structured thinking should be useful to take control of the situation without wasting time for analytical approach to the problems. I agree with Thompson & Martin to certain extend. However, I am not sure what happens if small businesses do not have any power of controlling Large & Medium Size Competitors (LMC) and their unethical practices such as taking over Small Businesses Market Share (SBMS) with unpleasant mechanism of getting them out of the system by blocking the flow of customers through bureaucratic obstacles which destroy SBMS.

I experienced disturbance in education industry as a small provider when I registered with a system named as DSA-QAG database. The system has been updated with the new administrators called 'need assessors' who control the flow of dyslexic students by assigning them to LMC but not small providers. I contacted some of the need assessors and disability teams at universities/colleges in the UK to make myself visible to them. There was no reply to my queries apart from one disability adviser from one of the universities letting me know that they provide support service to dyslexic students internally and don't use external providers which is not feasible if we consider the fact that 15% of student population in HE/FE is dyslexic. None of the universities/colleges has got adequate human resources to accommodate dyslexic students internally. The disability adviser chose to discourage me from outsourcing dyslexic students as she did not really want to share the market share even in the expense of neglecting dyslexic students' urgent need for external support provision. I met hundreds of dyslexic students making complaints about the insufficient support services without meeting their needs internally at universities/colleges. Some of the dyslexic students waited for the whole academic year as there was no specialist tutor/ specialist mentor to match their specific needs internally.

On some occasions, some of the dyslexic students did not get specialist mentors for 3 years while they were at universities/ colleges. I came to contact with one of the dyslexic students who waited for my service for 3 years. The new system is impossible to control externally. The internal team members are blocking dyslexic students so that disabled students cannot reach external support provision by themselves. My potential dyslexic students can't reach me directly even I am on the DSA-QAG register. I have lost my market share since need assessors are introduced to the system to block dyslexic students' movement; need assessors receive £700 government grant for a two-hour informal assessment. Occasionally, I receive an email from a need assessor asking me whether I would be interested in supporting a dyslexic student who lives outside London. It is not possible for me to travel to another city to deliver one-hour face-to-face support session to a dyslexic student. Then, I don't hear anything from any need assessor for six months or a year. I only speculate that need assessors are in contact with Large & Medium Corporates; they might even get a commission from them in order to refer dyslexic students directly to them but not to small providers like me.

Everyone in any business category regardless their sizes (LMS) should be able to survive. Market share shouldn't be controlled in the most unfair way which favors L/M size corporates and restricts the survival of small providers especially within education and health provision. As long as dyslexic students are diagnosed as dyslexic with their DSA entitlement letter for dyslexia support, they should be given a chance to choose their external providers. Otherwise, disabled students lose their autonomy. It is not fair on dyslexic students who are unable to select their own specialist tutor/mentor and wait for a long time to be assigned to independent providers after exhausting the bureaucratic procedures of being held down internally. If disabled students are able to exercise their legal rights, they should be free to select their own independent external providers without being blocked by the internal need assessors or disability teams at universities/colleges. Only then, the disability provision will be fairer and more effective that is also cost effective in terms of saving time, money and disabled students' energy which could be used for students' progress towards their learning outcomes instead.

Today's commercialism has been adulterated with aggressive selling tactics which are not in line with any spiritual belief system. When I read biblical stories, I am fascinated with the work ethics our Divine Creator set up for His creations. Today, I reread Exodus where there is a passage which depicts Moses's dialogue with his Creator. Moses was called to deliver the children of Israel, out of Egypt from the oppression of 430 years. Daily bread is described in a simple way which should be easily accessible without facing conspiracies and disturbances of all kind in business. Political leaders, LMS business owners and consumers need to accept the fact that everyone ought to have an equal access to market share without violating the Divine Law. The following quotes are from the second book of Moses named Exodus which is predicted to be written about 1400 B.C. According to the script, Moses name interpreted as "Drawn Out" and he is the Hebrew prophet who delivered the Israelites out of Egypt, to Mount of Sinai where they received God's law (Exodus, p. 82).

> *Then the Lord said to Moses, "Behold, I will rain bread from heaven for you. And the people shall go out and gather a certain quote every day, that I may test them, whether they will walk in My law or not.*
> **Exodus 16:4, The Holy Bible, NKJV, 1991, p. 106**

> *"This is the thing which the Lord has commanded: 'Let every man gather it according to each one's need, one omer for each person, according to the number of persons; let every man take for those who are in his tent.'"*
> **Exodus 16:16, The Holy Bible, NKJV, 1991, p. 106**

> *"Then the children of Israel did so and gathered, some more, some less.*
> **Exodus 16:17, The Holy Bible, NKJV, 1991, p. 106**

> *And Moses said, "Let no one leave any of it till morning."*
> **Exodus 16:19, The Holy Bible, NKJV, 1991, p. 107**

> *Notwithstanding they did not heed Moses. But some of them left part of it until morning, and it bred worms and stank. And Moses was angry with them.*
> **Exodus 16:20, The Holy Bible, NKJV, 1991, p. 107**

The human nature is fallible. Some individuals want more than they need and accumulate wealth which they will never be able to consume within the limitation of their lifetime while others go hungry and starve to death without any access to their share. We are all on trial being judged by our deeds daily. The more we listen to God's voice, the more we'll comply with God's divine judgement. Justice for all could be accomplished without compromise if only we kept on reading moral stories which provide us God's words about what is ethical and what is not as follows:

> *"You shall not circulate a false report. Do not put your hand with the wicked to be unrighteous witness.*
> **Exodus 23, Bible, NKJV, 1991, p. 115**

> *"You shall not follow a crowd to do evil; nor shall you testify in a dispute so as to turn aside after many to pervert justice.*
> **Exodus 23:2, Bible, NKJV, 1991, p. 115**

> *"You shall not show partiality to a poor man in his dispute.*
> **Exodus 23:3, Bible, NKJV, 1991, p. 115**

> *"You shall not pervert the judgement of your poor in his dispute.*
> **Exodus 23:6, Bible, NKJV, 1991, p. 115**

> *"Keep yourself far from a false matter; do not kill the innocent and righteous. For I will not justify the wicked.*
> **Exodus 23:7, Bible, NKJV, 1991, p. 115**

> *"And you shall take no bribe, for a bribe blinds the discerning and perverts the words of righteous.*
> **Exodus 23:8, Bible, NKJV, 1991, p. 115**

> *"Also, you shall not oppress a stranger, for you know the heart of a stranger, because you were strangers in the land of Egypt.*
> **Exodus 23:9, Bible, NKJV, 1991, p. 115**

Divine Justice takes an important part in our day-to-day business interactions even in the face of adversity caused to us by the unjust people when we are treated in an unfair way. Each exploitation, innocent people experience, will be restored by God's mercy eventually. The ultimate truth about Divine Justice is revealed in God's word as follows;

> *"God does not commit an atom's weight of injustice; and if there is a good deed, He doubles it, and gives from His presence a sublime compensation."*
> **Quran:40, Modern English Translation by Talal Itani, 2014**

> *"God does not guide the unjust people."*
> **Quran: 86, Modern English Translation by Talal Itani, 2014**

> *"God has permitted commerce and has forbidden usury."*
> **Quran: 275, Modern English Translation by Talal Itani, 2014**

I attended many court cases as part of my private research for a few years while I was writing my novel titled ***Dyslexia isn't an Obstacle***. In my fiction, my novel character, Felix faces injustice as a young dyslexic orphan. When his foster parents asked Felix to leave home, he experiences homelessness and commits a crime. Then, Felix faces a two-year imprisonment in jail where he finds the freedom of expression the first time in his life whilst learning reading and writing in order to get out of the poverty trap. I wanted to investigate the British Justice System in order to be able to elaborate fairness and unfairness in my literature work. Each court case I observed in the British Courtroom, the witness was asked to take an oath or make an affirmation as quoted below;

> "When you are called to give evidence, you will be shown to the witness box and be asked to stand. Before giving evidence in court you will be asked if you wish to take an oath or make an affirmation that your evidence is true. The difference between an oath and an affirmation is that the oath is a religious commitment whereas an affirmation is non-religious."

CROWN COURT WITNESS OATH

> "I swear by ... (according to religious belief) that the evidence I shall give shall be the truth the whole truth and nothing but the truth."

CROWN COURT WITNESS AFFIRMATION

> "I do solemnly, sincerely and truly declare and affirm that the evidence I shall give shall be the truth the whole truth and nothing but the truth."

> https://www.nidirect.gov.uk/articles/giving-evidence-court [accessed on 25 Apr 2018]

Once we are fully aware of what Divine Justice means by consulting the moral books first, it gets easier for us to make ethical choices between acceptable and unacceptable terms and conditions in business transactions. Business Wellbeing Coach encourages political leaders; large, medium, small business owners; consumers and citizens to look at their business relationships in the light of Divine Justice. Once our spiritual conscious is developed through regular ethical practices, it is not difficult to make better informed judgements. Ethical values are taken from the moral books such as Old Testament, New Testament and Quran which advocate fairness for all in commerce, education, health care, housing, employment and pension entitlement. Therefore, there is no room for any delusion whilst deciding what is ethical or unethical.

Are we getting there or not?

Today, I talked to an administrator to find out what the procedure was to report when the DSA-funded disabled students don't contact me for an unknown reason which is not possible for me to monitor due to the fact that some disabled students are unreachable. While we were discussing the matter over the phone, I sensed that there was not a certain procedure to follow. When there is not any formal procedure to follow, it becomes anything goes according to unpredictable crises which occur quite often under the competitive environment of Disability Provision including losing my potential clients due to the commercial espionage. Large and medium size competitors accuse small providers of stealing their customers from them; there isn't such an expression to use when large and medium size providers are stealing my potential students from me. At the end of my telephone enquiry about what is the norm in terms of fair competition within the DSA-QAG registered providers, I understood that large and medium corporates are permitted to compete with small providers using aggressive selling tactics and taking their small competitors' market share; whereas, small independent providers are not allowed to compete with large and medium corporates. The game of competition has got a double standard for different sizes of competitors which causes an unfair disadvantage for small independent providers.

I remember what went wrong with the Brexit negotiations since 2017 as two different points of view in terms of negotiating trade deals between the EU and the British public had been contradictory. British Brexit Negotiator, David Davis was reporting his experience as Cabinet minister during his meeting with Michel Barnier in Brussels to the journalists by saying that *'We're getting there'* while the EU representative Michel Barnier, as Chief Negotiator for the 27 EU countries was stating that *'We're not getting there yet.'* It is a matter of different opinions and deals in terms of what is acceptable for one negotiator which may not be acceptable for the other one if deals are not based on equality and fairness.

Today, I checked the most up-to-date news about Brexit deals online to see whether or not Brexit deal has been negotiated by both parties fairly enough. I've found the following comment.

> *Angela Merkel has mocked Theresa May's Brexit negotiating tactics, saying the two leaders end up going around in circles because Mrs May never says what she wants.*
>
> *The German Chancellor said that whenever she asks the Prime Minister what she wants from the EU, she always replies: "Make me an offer."*
>
> *"But you're leaving - we don't have to make you an offer. Come on, what do you want?" Mrs May then repeats: "Make me an offer."*
>
> Gordon Rayner, Political Editor, 29 Jan 2018

Thompson & Martin (2010) suggest the essential steps in changing culture, accepting and diagnosing the existing culture by spotting any weaknesses besides highlighting the magnitude of the need for change in their book entitled *Strategic Management, Awareness & Change.*

> *"Lewin (1947) contends that there are three important stages in the process of change: unfreezing existing behaviour, changing attitudes and behaviour and refreezing the new behaviour as accepted common practice."*
>
> *as cited in Thompson & Martin, 2010, p.248*

Decision makers should be willing to make equivalent compromises when they look at the problems faced by all concerned. If there was no identical compromise, the outcome would be unsatisfactory for large, medium and small providers at the end of any unethical aggressive competition. I'd like to keep my market share whilst large and medium corporates are aiming to take over my share, for instance. I am constantly pushed out of the Disability Provision which is large enough for small independent providers to survive. When I looked back to our ancestors' philosophy of survival, I recognized the importance of getting things right first time to avoid a waste of resources as any error would be too costly in terms of human sacrifices for their daily survival.

> *"A voyage of a thousand miles begins with a single step. It is important that that step is in the right direction."*
>
> Old Chinese saying *as cited in Thompson & Martin, 2010, p.266*

Whistleblowing at work

Definition of whistleblowers and their legal rights are identified on government website as follows:

> *"You're a whistleblower if you're a worker and you report certain types of wrongdoing. This will usually be something you've seen at work."*
>
> *"The wrongdoing you disclose must be in the public interest. This means it must affect others, e.g. the general public."*
>
> *"As a whistleblower, you're protected by law – you shouldn't be treated unfairly or lose your job because you 'blow the whistle."*
>
> **https://www.gov.uk/whistleblowing [accessed on 01 Feb 2018]**

According to Whistleblowing Guidance for Employers and Code of Practice (2015, p.7), it is not enough for organizations to have a whistleblowing policy in place without training employees on how the policy should be implemented in practice. If transparency is promoted through whistleblowing policy within any organization in the UK, managers and business leaders need to create an open culture which should encourage employees to speak up about any wrongdoing they witness without being penalized such as facing job loss through unfair dismissal. Whistleblowing Guidance (2015, p.10) also gives guidelines to the managers who deal with whistleblowing concerns about how to protect personal information when it is disclosed in order to demonstrate best practice without breaching confidentiality.

The senior Risk Manager at HBOS, Paul Moore was unfairly dismissed when he raised his concerns about the high level of exposure for public investment as dangerous to James Crosby who was the bank's CEO in 2009. Moore's concern was not recorded at the Board meeting.

> ...Paul Moore, head of group regulatory risk at HBOS in 2002-05, to set out his allegations that he had been repeatedly threatened after claiming internally that the bank was "going too fast", "had a cultural indisposition to challenge" and "was a serious risk to financial stability and consumer protection".
>
> The Guardian Newspaper, 2009

When I examined the background of James Crosby as the former Chief Executive of HBOS, who sacked Paul Moore by breaching whistleblowing guidelines, I couldn't identify the weakness of his educational record. James Crosby was educated at the Lancaster Royal Grammar School from 1967 to 1974. Then, he completed a degree in mathematics at Brasenose College, Oxford. However, Crosby's degree in maths didn't enable him to predict possible weaknesses of exposure to high risk investments with public money. Crosby appointed as managing director of Halifax bank in 1994 and managed to move to the 1st Chief Executive of brand new HBOS Group as soon as being merged between Halifax plc and the Bank of Scotland in 2001.

After seven years of working as Chief Executive Crosby leaves HBOS Group in 2006. Crosby was banned from financial sector after being found responsible for the collapse of HBOS in 2008 which caused wiping out shareholders with £20.5 billion taxpayer bailout (BBC News, 2013). James Crosby admits his errors BBC Radio 4 as recorded below:

> *"If we are fortunate, the cost of the crises will be paid by our children. More likely it will still be being paid for by our grandchildren."*

According to Guardian Newspaper (2013), James Crosby handed back 30% of his £580,000 annual pension; yet, Crosby is still able to get £406,000 pension each year for his retirement which is 80 times more than the average private sector employee's income at mature age. James Crosby was not penalised for his errors as he was allowed to take a large sum of pension when 32,000 employees lost their jobs because of the merger between HBOS and Lloyds. Fairness has not been experienced equally well between James Crosby and redundant employees at mature age. James Crosby appears to be the winner in an economic sense while the redundant employees are being perceived as the losers at the end of the financial disaster. Probably, none of the redundant employees would want to be in Crosby's place as human integrity means more than millions.

I wonder whether the subject Work Ethics was introduced to James Crosby when he was studying maths at university as part of course curriculum. If he was introduced to Work Ethics during his studies, how he assimilated the topic at that time. Regrettably, Crosby did not implement the theory in practice during his working career! Crosby did not pay any attention to his colleague Paul Moore's warning for minimising risk with public money. Furthermore, Crosby couldn't bear to see Moore around and sacked him so that he would not have any whistleblower around to bother his guilt conscious.

Paul Moore sued HBOS for his unfair dismissal; thanks to the whistle blowing legislation as he was also the Good Practice Manager for whistleblowing at HBOS. However, some of the whistleblowers do not have an access to an important position Paul Moore had. Information is the most powerful asset to defend employees' rights to protect their professional integrity when serious offence takes place. What happened to professionals who felt responsible to warn their seniors to correct their wrong doings within any industry? Many employees are not knowledgeable their legal obligation to raise their concerns in order to restore ethical work practice. If they do raise their concerns, they lose their job security for life. The majority of the workplaces do not have whistleblowing policy in place in the UK. Business Wellbeing Coach encourages employees and employers to be transparent in order to restore a good practice at workplace without feeling threatened by anybody including their employers.

I remember one of my BA students facing an ethical dilemma at her placement during her architectural studies in 2017. She was asked to sketch the given space at her university and come up with a creative solution of re-using the narrow corridor effectively. While she was doing her practical research, she realised that the fire door wasn't designed properly. In the case of fire, the fire door would cause health hazard as smoke could enter the narrow corridor. The student was too hesitant to raise her concern as she did not want to cause any problem to the profession who designed the faulty fire door. I encouraged the student to record her finding in her professional development diary as it is an important diagnosis of the faulty design structure. A few months later, there was Grenfell Tower tragedy which shocked the general public as many residents lost their lives because of the negligence of professionals. If one person dared to point out the faulty structure of Grenfell Tower during the inspection process of the health and safety regulation, the disaster could be prevented. Most of the time, raising professional concerns is a matter of life and death issue and should be encouraged accordingly with a positive approach without victimising whistle blowers so harshly. My poem depicts how I feel when life gets harder as an outsider in our strange world.

Open Asylum

life became an open asylum in this century
with oppressors, fraud companies, terrorists of all types
threatening our human dignity on a daily basis
the crazy pop-up advertisements
the news with tragic consequences of crime on the media
corruption in banking, education, health care and politics
beggars, homeless, unemployed in every corner of the city
fraud companies look for more victims to trap
stock exchange collapses in London
employment market breeds hatred and unfair competition
nothing is secured for today let alone tomorrow
the long-term deficit is unrecoverable for at least another decade
sirens of police cars, ambulance and fire brigades continue without ceasing
fumes from the cars and central heating cover the atmosphere
pedestrians have no oxygen to breath in and out
hunger is experienced by the starving poor
hackers of ransom malware increase the cybercrime
unbroken promises up in the air
the cost of life is on the increase

so are the unfair dismissals
market share drops below zero
noise of bullies and naggers
obsessions with money, blood, sex and aggressive political power
life is turned into an open prison
with dangerous inmates on the run
nothing seems normal any longer
the only normality is my sanity
amongst all the eccentricities of this century
yet, I know I am not one of them
I am innocent without any obsessive mentality
free from the mind of criminal identity
free from the manias of this century
my freedom keeps me away from the irrationality
without any doubt for my ambition to stay uninvolved with crimes
nothing decent is left for the innocents to occupy with
my spiritual journey gives me the inner peace each day
with a courage to be myself
my spiritual identity is my strength
in an open asylum
without losing my hope for a better future

© **Firdevs Dede**
03 Feb 2018, London

Human nature is unpredictable

A mature student with family commitment was referred to me on 16th Feb 2017 by the DSA-QAG registered need assessor. I met the student on 1st March 2017. She was having a dilemma between the long distance of the university in another city where she was going to study nursing and her family commitments where she originally lived. The student told me the difficulties she was facing and asked my patience for the situation. I didn't hear from her for a while. When I made enquiries whether or not she was available to attend her 2nd support session, I was confronted by her unpredictable behavior. Although she booked me for 13th Apr 2017, she didn't make an effort to attend the second session or felt any need to give me any feedback why she changed her mind for not attending the session. I still kept in touch with the mature student via text messages hoping that she recovered from her unpredictable mood swing and would show the sign of commitment to her support sessions which didn't happen. Professor Katherine Hawley (2015) in her paper titled *Trust and Distrust between Patient and Doctor* underlines the concept of trust within health sector as follows:

> ...trust is rarely a one-way street, and there are also important questions about the degree to which doctors can or should trust their patients...
>
> In any discussion of trust and distrust, however, it is useful to bear in mind the risks associated with miscommunication about what can reasonably expected of either party: misplaced trust can be a dangerous thing for both truster and trustee.
>
> Professor Katherine Hawley (2015), p.8

When I heard from the same provider for another referral on 24 Jan 2018, I made enquiries about the mature student studying nursing who was referred to me in 2017. I was told that she requested for a change of supplier in Apr 2017 at the time she booked me for the 2nd support session. I was puzzled and hurt by the student's misconduct as she didn't give me a reason for her unpredictable behavior. I didn't want to waste my time with the unpredictable nature of the complicated student and I accepted the new student's referral. I sent the new student the 1st contact email with my timetable for arranging her support session on 24 Jan 2018. I didn't get any reply to my email and text messages. I thought it was another negative experience. I was willing to forget about the new student. Then, I heard from the new student on 1st Feb 2018 as she called me and explained the reason why she couldn't contact me. We agreed to meet on Monday 5th Feb 2018 in the public library. The first snow of the winter fell down on the date when my new learner arrived with her trolley. We spent 2 and a ½ hrs to discuss her needs for her face-to-face support sessions. The new student seemed to be happy to meet me and she was keen to work with me. The law student booked her 2nd session immediately as she sounded serious to meet her deadlines for the 5 assignments in legal studies she failed previously. She told me that she does a part time agency work as a speech therapist for an autistic child although the agency work was erratic, she warned me about her inflexible working hours. On the same day, she called me and explained that her agency asked her to work for Wednesday and couldn't meet me on Wednesday. She asked me to reschedule the session for Friday which I did without any hard feeling. On Friday 9th Feb 2018, I went to the public library very early to make sure we would have a table to place the learning material. Additionally, I booked a PC as she didn't have a laptop to bring. I settled in for a good working day. The law student sent a text message telling me that she couldn't make it because she was called by the agency to work on Friday. It was 10:30 am. I was upset by the two cancellations in the same week. However, I didn't have any choice but to leave the library. I sent an email and text messages to the new learner explaining the cancellation policy and rescheduled her support session to Tuesday 13th Feb 2018 as she had to go to university and couldn't take a day off for her agency work. I didn't hear from the new student at weekends, Monday and Tuesday. I understood that the new student had the problem with time management without getting her priorities right. I gave myself a week before drawing my final conclusion whether or not she would benefit from support sessions. In the case of not hearing from any student for an indefinite period, the working relationship with a student usually deteriorates. Students' irregular attendance pattern won't benefit either them or myself as a support tutor/mentor. A machine language operates with a binary numerical system which is based on zero and one (0 and 1) code; whereas, a human language operates with a system based on one-to-one (1 to 1) interaction which brings a meaningful learning experience with relevant discussions on each topic we engage with.

Business Wellbeing Coach sets achievable priorities for human concerns with specific problems such as not being able to commit oneself to important tasks. If a client neglects 100% commitment to their priorities, the outcome is usually unpleasant which might even cause the same patterns of negativity in the case of failing the 5 assignments over again. A client needs to attend their sessions regularly with the intention of making a steady progress in their learning and applying all the strategies to practice. Without practicing wellbeing strategies, a client is unable to adopt new ways of thinking, doing and achieving the standard which they failed to fulfil previously over the course of their academic life or business life. It is a matter of firm decision each client needs to make about whether or not they really want to make a good progress in their lives. It is not possible for anybody even with the highest IQ to reach where they want to get without committing to their original plans which have been outlined and agreed at each session. That is why I always stress the importance of my priority in my coaching, mentoring and teaching practice which is 100 percent of commitment on both sides. It is not enough for me to commit to the client's achievement when they do not demonstrate the same commitment I expect from them to invest to their one-to-one sessions. If we look at any learning practice from the perspective of a return on investment value, there is nothing which might be returned without being invested first. Therefore, a client needs to invest their time and energy to their support program in order to reap the benefit of their investment in the short-term or long-term period. Any learning process with a full commitment will bring growth not only in our personal development but in our financial stability for survival within the competitive environment of a work force which constantly increases its demands on employees' capability to make a steady progress without regression. Wasting time means wasting money in the long run over the working life-span of each employee. Not being able to focus on the core skills such as prioritizing tasks, time management and organizational skills for increasing each employee's survival, will ultimately slow down their progress to fill the gap within the skilled and unskilled workforce for the economic growth besides delaying a possible job satisfaction. The tragedy occurs when human workforce waste time, talent, potential of employees without reaching satisfactory outcomes at the end of each decade. It is inevitable that robots will be taking over human workforce eventually. The winners will be still around with 100 percent of commitment to development of their core skills to share robotic workforce without being redundant from the employment market. To continue or not to continue at the age of machinery is the first question to ask oneself for our daily survival! The second question begs for an answer.

How could you continue to survive without core skills?

There is no correct answer which might eliminate the second question's irrationality. The rational answer is that there is no possibility of survival without core skills in a machine age with robotic workmates around. Therefore, I am still hopeful to get students who are willing to survive in a machine age and are able to commit themselves to their sessions regularly in order to increase their capability beyond the immediacy of the current time which promises more cash value in the long-run.

Special Days – 21 Feb 2018

Two special days make us to be recognized as a numerical value in life. I believe, our birthday is as important as our departure day from this life. Today is 21st Feb 2018 which is my birthday. It feels good to be remembered on my birthday.

I liked receiving birthday messages from my students who I met 37 years ago when I was a young graduate employed as a secondary school teacher. My students who sent me birthday wishes are both grownups with their adult children. One of them is a retired civil servant; the other one is still working as an MP in Turkey. It was good to receive a birthday message from my colleague, our science teacher who I met 37 years ago in the same village school in the northern part of Turkey. The total number of the students was one hundred which made our teaching life more caring when we were able to know each student more than the students at city schools with overcrowded student population. It was equally surprising to receive a birthday message from a new friend who I met on my cruise trip to Europe in Dec 2017. We took each other's photos. She kindly sent me her birthday wishes with a photo she took on the cruise ship via social media.

I lived longer than half a century. I hope that I will have extra fulfilling years ahead of me to visit some more cities, to meet honest people and to accumulate some more enjoyable memories long after my retirement. What makes my life is worthwhile is that the unfinished journey from one country to another. My life is a gift from God as all the cities I visit are God's creation. The human beings, animals, plants, trees are the living art forms of our Divine Creator. I often remember of those unborn babies who were abandoned in their mothers' womb without any chance given to them to experience this beautiful life with its meaningful human relationships. How sad I feel each time to remember the loss of unborn children via abortion. I wish our Creator's human creations had given a fair right to enter this world and feel its greatness without any sabotage to their human existence.

I often pray for the unborn babies' spiritual wellbeing. How painful it must have been for the healthy babies to be aborted by their maternal parents' decision when they were deprived from compassion and genuine parental love for their wellbeing. I consider myself a very lucky person being born and bred within a loving family background and reaching my mature age with a great satisfaction. When I look back to my life history, it looks like a day or two on a holiday resort which I don't want to cease because of its blessings such as good weather, delicious food, hospitable surroundings, beautiful animals and very compassionate people with kindness and caring attitude to make me feel I am welcome.

One of my students went back to her birth country seven months ago. We met on Skype last Sunday and reflected on her life with her family being brought up in another country as a child; spending her youth in London; then, going back to her birth country. The city she lives now is a very historical city with God's blessings such as beautiful weather; the red sea and the holiness of non-stop praying coming from the residents and visitors of the city. I didn't consider taking a long fly journey to visit Jeddah, Mecca and Medina before. After being invited to visit my student who did her dissertation on Islamic Architecture and Arts, I've decided to go to Saudi Arabia in the near future. Our time is very limited. We don't know exactly when we are going to reach the end of the road. It's always good to make fast decisions without delaying certain journeys while we are still alive as each journey enriches our spiritual wellbeing when we are connected to our mutual ancestors and observe the passing history within the architectural structures of the old cities which have survived the centuries just like human beings. Business Wellbeing Coach encourages clients to be more authentic in their decision-making process when they listen to God's calling for special journeys to mature spiritually through experiencing the surroundings of holiness whenever an opportunity arises.

A day after my birthday, I wanted to give a chance to my new student who has stopped replying to my emails; I texted her another message. My new student's ancestors come from Africa and she studies law in London. I remember her attending the initial session in a public library. We had the first snow of the year. I watched the beautiful snow falling down gracefully from the French window in the library before her arrival. The new student of mine arrived in her long overcoat. I felt I was experiencing something unusual and appreciated her special effort to attend her initial session in the freezing cold and very early morning without having enough time to have her breakfast at home. She sat down and started biting her sandwich to stop her hunger before talking about herself. She looked a promising committed student. We spent 2 and a ½ hours discussing her needs, how she wanted to progress in her life. She even called me and told me it was good to meet me. All of a sudden, she stopped replying to my email and text messages. Yesterday, reflecting on my good relationships with my students, colleagues and some of my friends who kindly remembered my birthday without expecting me to remember theirs in return, I thought I shouldn't give up on this young law student and texted her the following note.

> Hello …
>
> I hope all is well with you.
>
> I'd appreciate if you could give me feedback why you've stopped communicating with me.
>
> Just think about yourself and your clients. What would happen if they stopped responding to your correspondence without any reason? Would you just ignore them or keep on finding the answer of their silence?
>
> In coaching, it's important to complete each relation with dignity without hurting anybody.
>
> I look forward to hearing from you soon.
>
> Best regards,
> Firdevs Dede
> Support Tutor/Mentor
> 22 Feb 2018

If we are unable to communicate with the people who care about us, the communication process with the uncaring people would be impossible. That is why building up a very good foundation of a two-way communication process with our clients, friends, family members, employers, employees and fellow human beings is the most important skill to be mastered over the years within our finite life span. Otherwise, there will be plenty of broken relationships without a heartfelt goodbye to each other in a good spirit. Our life is a journey. Once we leave this life, the only precious things will be staying behind us that are the meaningful memories of the people who cared for our wellbeing. It is easy to hurt anyone in life but it is not easy to be considerate. Remembering our fragile mortality will help us to be more kind to ourselves which allow us to give a chance to others and hope that they use their given allowances to treat us in the way how we want to be treated with kindness, unlimited positive regards and unconditional love. Unfortunately, in conventional life expectations, people act more judgmental than they really think they are when it comes to decision making process about others' behaviors as they completely ignore the sensitivity of the people who care about them.

I watched the sad news on TV soon after my birthday while the Russians killed civilians in Syria. There was a father with his dead son covered in plastic bag. It was unbelievable tragic scene. He must have been going through trauma while he was holding his son's corpse. There was no time for the distressed father to mourn when there was nowhere to bury his dead son. According to the BBC (23 Feb 2018), the dead toll has risen to 462 in Syria and at least 99 of them are children. Barrel bombs and shell fire have filled the area where 393,000 civilians are trapped. We are living in a dreadful time of manmade horror and misery. I wonder when there will be universal peace without any war taking place anywhere on this earth. Time is running out for compassion, kindness and forgiveness. Human life is turned into a merciless tragedy. Let's pray for the end of the political conflicts when politicians are incapable of resolving human tragedies peacefully!

Miraculous events do occur as well as cynical ones in life!

One of the most celebrated British Professor of Mathematics, Stephen Hawking passed away peacefully aged 76 on 14 March 2018 (Guardian, 2018). The British Media announced the sad news besides other sad news such as the rising rate of the death toll among the young people who bought slimming pills over the Internet and died from 'Lethal' DNP diet pills. Stephen Hawking led a fulfilling life despite the fact that he suffered from incurable motor neuron condition since he was 21 years old. The doctors predicted that he would live for 2 years only. Although the physical quality of his life had gradually deteriorated, Professor Hawking had never lost his optimism, wit and his appetite for longer life. Hawking made the most of his life without mourning about the life-threatening disease he endured over the 55 years life-span. The commentators who knew Stephen Hawking emphasized his sense humor and how much he enjoyed his glamorous career. Stephen Hawking had married to two beautiful women at different periods of his life. More importantly, he saw himself rather handsome, loveable and respectable person as he did not have any doubt about his attraction.

I read Jim Blythe's categories of self-concept in his book titled *Consumer Behaviour* as noted below;

> *"Real self is objective self how others see us.*
> *Self-image is how we see ourselves.*
> *Ideal self is how we wish we were.*
> *Looking-glass self is the social self who we think how other people perceive us.*
> *Possible selves are the selves we wish we could become."*

Jim Blythe, 2013, p.90

I thought the scientist Stephen Hawking's real self was not different than his other selves such as ideal self and looking-glass self. He had also reached his possible selves when he expanded his professional identity to his life-long research studies. I believe that Professor Hawking accomplished his 76 years long life journey with professional and personal satisfaction of being accepted and respected as he appeared worldwide without necessarily seeking for others' acknowledgement. I wonder how much happier Hawking could have been if he had worked on his spiritual identity which he neglected. Professor Hawking quite bluntly admitted that there is no life beyond this life in his own words stated below:

> *"I regard the brain as a computer which will stop working when its components fail," he said. "There is no heaven or afterlife for broken-down computers; that is a fairy story for people afraid of the dark."*

Guardian, 2018

I can't help feeling sad for Hawking's departure without having any comfort of sensing another dimension of his life here and now while he was alive. Nevertheless, I feel such a relief that

Steven Hawking will be experiencing a pleasant surprise when he finally meets his Creator in heaven. No one really knows what will happen when our spirits leave our bodies, where our spirits go to and how our spirits experience after life existence. Unlike metaphysical scientists, moral skeptic scientists under the influence of logical positivism are unable to connect to any form of spiritual reality by missing out on the beautiful dream of spiritual realm beyond the physical existence of the earth. I wish Hawking had included a spiritual self to his possible selves when he was still alive before setting out on his final journey to infinity.

My spiritual belief reveals that Stephen Hawking won't be perished because he was unable to connect to God's existence in a spiritual way due to his biased conditioning within the limitation of the human knowledge. I sense that Hawking was born to fulfil God's mission to prove the medical doctors wrong when he was granted with extra 55 years despite the incurable disease he was diagnosed with in his early 20s. Our Creator keeps reminding us that human reasoning is fallible and it is not possible for most of us to predict God's purposes for His creations.

I did a bit of research on the victims of 'Lethal' DNP diet pills on the same day Hawking passed away peacefully in silence. I found the saddest news about the beautiful victim, Sara Houston who was ironically a medical student when she was seeking to reach her ideal self. Despite her medical academic background, she was secretly taking slimming pills which she purchased online and died in Sept 2012 (BBC, 2012). Sara looks strikingly beautiful in her photo. What made Sara feel unsatisfactory with her appearance is a mystery to me! Could it be a peer pressure to attain size zero? Could it be the aggressive selling techniques of unethical salespeople with pop-up advertisements on social media while Sara was surfing online?

According to BBC (2016), the Medicine and Healthcare Products Regulatory Agency (MHRA) detained £1.4 million worth of unlicensed dietary medicine in 2015-16, £960,000 more than two years earlier. Senior policy manager, Lynda Scammell at the MHRA explains the grim reality of the slimming pills with 2,4-dinitrophenol or DNP which is a highly toxic industrial chemical and is not intended for human consumption as stated below;

> *"The Internet offers access to a vast number of websites offering products marketed as 'slimming' or 'diet' pills. Many of these pills will not be licensed medicines. That means their contents are unknown and untested."*
>
> Lynda Scammell, 2016

How immoral it is to make money out of selfish desire in the expense of damaging consumers' health and causing their premature death! A person with a matured spiritual identity foresees the negative consequences of any unethical business transaction and avoids the life-threatening results which could be in conflict with their spiritual integrity. Therefore, Business Wellbeing Coach is for everybody to distinguish the difference between spiritual satisfaction and materialistic dissatisfaction during any business transaction as BWC always treats consumers under the spiritual awareness of God's authority. Our spiritual conscious should be in charge when confronted by the greed of animal instinct in order to make ethical decisions to keep customers safe without damaging their wellbeing physically, mentally, spiritually and financially.

Numerical Values

I remember of explaining my numeracy students the importance of gaining numeracy skills in life as some of my students hated numbers while I was working as a numeracy teacher and internal assessor for OCR vocational training in 2005 in the UK. I gave my 16-year-old students tangible examples from everyday context. There is a numerical value in everything we get to know from the very beginning to the very end, I said. Our birthday is a numerical value. We read calendars in numerical expression such as weeks; months; years and time is measured daily by numbers with 24 hrs. We use numerical values in the exchange of any business transaction. We earn money when we buy or sell products and services. Our skills and work experience are measured with a numerical value. We get wages or salary with a numerical value weekly or monthly. Many people judge one another in accordance with how much they are worth with tangible and intangible assets they posses during their life time. We measure ingredients while we cook. Our body size is measured by dressmakers or tailors. We know our height and weight by using numerical values. We measure furniture to predict whether or not each piece fits into our environment at home or in office. Our address has got a door number, a street number, a local area code. We dial phone numbers. We count people for the estimation of human population. We measure weather conditions with numbers. We assess consumers' satisfaction feedback with a rating scale of 1 to 10. Scientists predict the age of earth with numerical expressions. Educators measure students' capability with a marking system which has got a numerical value from failure, to pass or distinction. Doctors take patients' blood pressure; check heart rate and interpret the numbers to us as high or low. Any deficiency in our metabolism is identified with a specific numerical value. How much calorie an average male and female should be taking has been identified with numbers. The inflation rate is a numerical expression and identified by analysts. Our profit & loss account appears in numbers. Statistical findings represent numbers. We get connected to our well-known ancestors in the human history predicting what age they were from stone age to industrial ages. We would like to know our ancestors' life-span in order to figure out the average human life. Some people have their lucky numbers to play lottery. We remember our passwords in digits for credit cards transactions. Our National Insurance Number is a combination of several digits and letters. We are given a membership number when we join professional organizations. Finally, when we die, the date is recorded alongside our birthday. We are valued numerically with the time span we appeared and disappeared from this earth. Students ID number is unique for each student. For example, the first five years of my primary education I was connected to number 2 as my primary school ID number was 2. Then, I had three years connection to the number 781 as my secondary school ID number.

When I was doing my MA degree in fine art printmaking, I developed a concept called *'Triangularity of Thought'* and I titled the series of my prints as *Triangularity of Thought* which appealed many audience in 1990s. I was often asked what I meant with *Triangularity of Thought*. My fine art prints were sold because of the images I produced in my prints were all triangle beings. The shape of triangle has attracted my imagination since geometry was introduced to me at secondary school. I remember one of the visitors whom I didn't know personally wanted to buy a couple of my prints *Triangularity of Thought 1* and *Triangularity of Thought 2 during* my final year exhibition. The irony was that there was *"not for sale"* notice underneath of each print I exhibited. Despite its strange notification, I was asked to sell my prints to the special guest who loved the idea of *Triangularity of Thought*. When I decided to give him the prints as my present, he insisted on paying me towards its cost at least. The person who bought my prints became a very good friend of mine until he passed away in 1993. He told me that *"Thought is abstract and triangle is abstract. I like the idea of its combination. Yes, thought could be a triangle."* We both have a good laugh in an Italian restaurant in Chiswick near Botanic Garden in Richmond where I delivered my prints to him personally.

In 2013, I set up my first enterprise titled *Three Dimension Dyslexia.* Some people asked me why I named my enterprise with the number three. I gave them my pragmatic answer because I offer three different services to dyslexic students as I tutor, mentor and coach them; that is why I cooperated them all in my trade name. I avoided the additional explanation about *"Dimension"* which is connected to sculpting. Because of my background as a visual artist, I am familiar with the concept that drawing is categorized as 2-dimensional activity whereas sculpting is defined as a 3-dimensional activity. When I teach, mentor and coach, each action depends on mutual interaction within either a face-to-face environment or a virtual environment which is not a monologue in the same way I write a book. It is a dialogue with participants such as students acting like thinking sculptures within an educational space which I call third-dimension.

In year 2017, I decided to set up my second enterprise which is titled *Business Wellbeing Coach – Unity of Hexagons*. I assume that I'll be asked the same odd question – why do you call your enterprise Hexagon? The idea came to me as I did a lot of research on geometrical patterns while I was on a textile course in 2003. I used a lot of hexagons in my textile images as many hexagons are found in the pattern of honey combs. I thought it would be fantastic if all our contribution to community work for our survival has been appreciated by one another which would bring a distinctive unity to our fragmented human existence within the global platform.

Today, I read Dr. David A. Phillips's book titled '*The Complete Book of Numerology, Discovering the Inner Self*' which was published in 2009. The author was born in 1934 and died in 1993 at the age of 59. While I am writing my book titled *Business Wellbeing Coach – Unity of Hexagons,* I am also 59 years old. It was such a sad discovery that I didn't read this interesting book when I was working on my fine art prints with all forms of geometrical shapes in early 1990s. It would have made such an impact on my interpretation of geometrical shapes I used in my fine art prints if I had an access to Dr. Phillips's knowledge of numbers. I realized once more that great writers survive beyond their limited life span. Dr. Phillips is still able to pass his knowledge on to me with his published book 25 years later his departure from this life. After reading Dr. Philips's explanation from Chapter 3 – *A Metaphysical Understanding of Numbers,* it is easier to interpret the importance of the special numbers my life has been shaped by so far.

> "Two is the first spiritual (feeling) number. It represents the duality of humans and symbolizes the gateway to

> *our sensitivities, as well as our need to be part of a pair. It is the number of intuition."*
>
> Dr. Phillips, 1992, p.7

I understand now why I liked my primary school ID number 2 during my schooling years for 5 years. It is the number of intuition. My life is based on intuitive discoveries including discovering Dr. Phillips's book on numerical values while I was finalizing my manuscript for its publication on 07 Apr 2018.

> *Three is the first mind (thinking) number. Following the primary verbal (1) and intuitive (2) expressions comes the mental. It is the gateway to the conscious mind and to rational understanding, the focus of left-brain activity, the key to memory. The number 3 is symbolized by the triangle, representing the connection of mind, soul and body.*
>
> Dr. Phillips, 1992, p.7

The name of my first enterprise *Three Dimension Dyslexia* has got a very meaningful connotation with the triangle representing the connection of mind, soul and body. Most of my dyslexic students' cognitive profile is based on intuition & creativity that represents right-brain approach. When I work with my dyslexic students, I introduce them academic reading & writing strategies which activate their left-brain for logical thinking via linguistic exercises.

The symbol of my logo for *Business Wellbeing Coach, Unity of Hexagon* is a six-sided polygon. When I mentor students and clients who are under a very demanding business environment, they experience daily worries, stress, anxiety and mild depression temporarily. I usually feel each person's negative energy which could be transferred into a positive and constructive creativity with spiritual exercises. The spiritual exercises I've included in this book are aimed to activate readers' inner spiritual-self in order to be happier and more satisfied with what we have got rather than what we lack of. I'd like to evaluate my findings with the following statement from Dr. Phillips.

> *"Six is the center of the mind (thinking) plane, where it represents creativity, the integration of the left and right lobes of the brain. It also represents the opposite of creativity – destruction. This is "negative" creativity expressed as worry, stress, anxiety and depression."*
>
> Dr. Phillips, 1992, p.7

How grand it is to find a supportive quote from Pythagoras about the purpose of my book titled 'Unity of Hexagons' in Dr. Philips's book (Chapter 7, p. 80) as follows!

> *"Evolution is the law of life*
> *Number is the law of the universe*
> *Unity is the law of God."*
>
> Pythagoras, as quoted by Edouard Schure in his book The Great Initiates

I expect that the readers who are lucky enough to read my book before moving to our eternal place, especially the ones who didn't have any chance to be connected to their spiritual consciousness previously will be expanding the limitation of their mortality beyond this life. Consequently, dying and bearing the physical losses of deceased love ones will be less painful.

Let's start your day with wellbeing exercises to increase your spiritual awareness of your spiritual uniqueness which would bring happiness and fulfilment in your daily life!

DAY 1

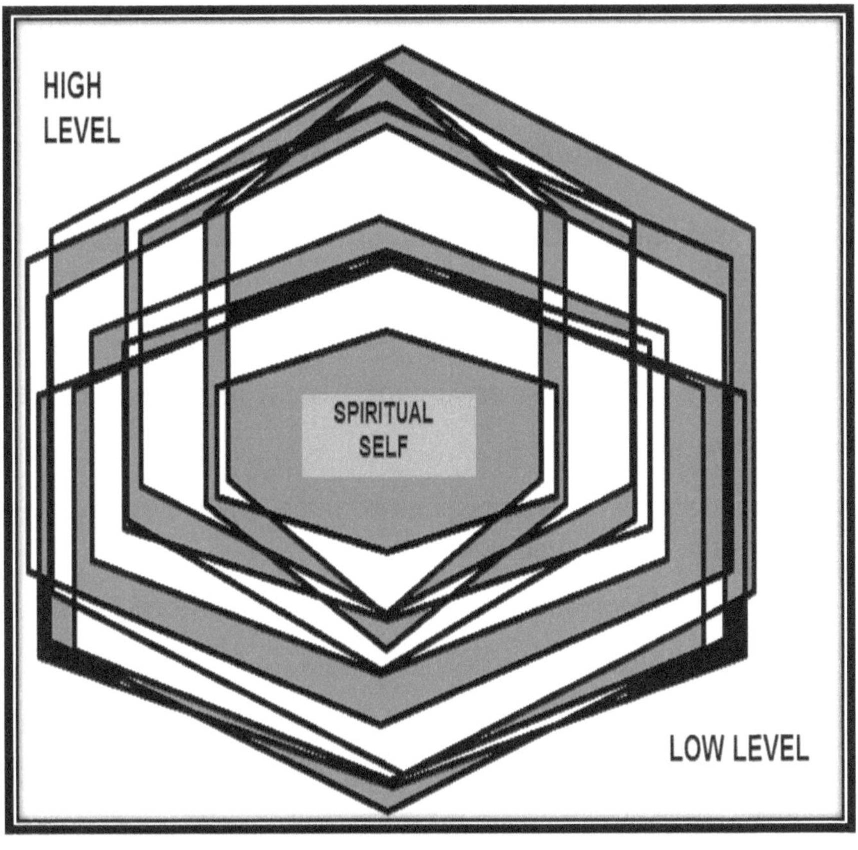

STAGE 1, © Firdevs Dede

What level of awareness are you experiencing in your spiritual identity?

Ask yourself what you understand from Spiritual Identity?

1) **Are you aware of who you are in terms of your spiritual beliefs?**

    a) Yes

    b) No

    c) Not sure

2) **How do you identify your spiritual awareness?**

    a) I was born and brought up within a faithful family background.

    b) I observe a certain formal religious practice.

    c) I have never taken any interest in any religious practice.

    d) I am nihilist.

    e) I am against all the religious dogmas which divide human beings and cause destruction.

    f) I am in favor of building up my personal moral code.

    g) I hate religious people's judgmental values.

    h) I feel I am not materialistic in a non-religious way but I lack the commitment and passion for building up a spiritual identity.

    i) I do not understand how it feels to have a spiritual identity.

    j) I am brought up to discard all forms of religious beliefs which cause hatred and divisions among believers.

    k) I'd like to explore possibilities that I'd increase my spiritual intelligence and wisdom for fulfilling the void in me.

DAY 1

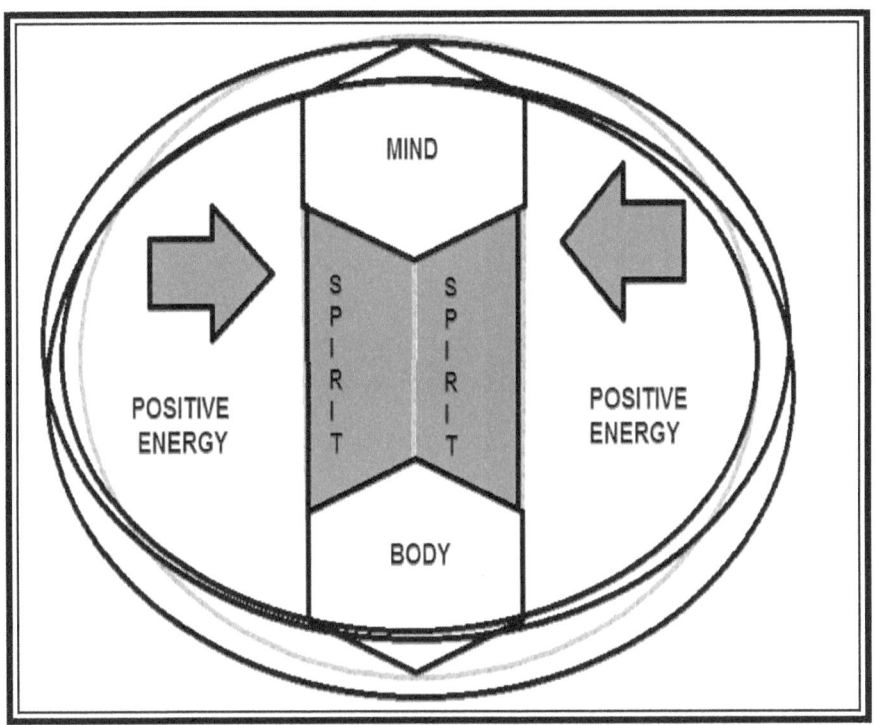

STAGE 2, © Firdevs Dede

Identifying the positive energy within your body, spirit, mind and all the things you are surrounded with.

1) **Are you aware of positive energy within you now?**

    a) Yes

    b) No

    c) Not sure

2) **How do you identify positive energy in your body, mind and spirit?**

    a) When I feel life is worth living, I know precisely that the positive energy is shaping my life.

    b) I am influenced by the positive thoughts in my body, mind and spirit.

    c) When I am optimist, I know that healing energy is active in my body and mind.

    d) I am fine with positive energy in the context of body and mind only.

    e) I am not sure about positive energy in a spiritual context.

    f) Positive energy in a spiritual context has never occurred to me.

    g) I am full of negativity which prevents me from positive thoughts.

    h) I feel a negative environment causes me negativity and I am a product of my destructive environment at home, work and community.

    i) Positive thoughts and actions scare me.

    j) I am comfortable with the daily misery I am used to.

    k) I am not sure what positive energy means really.

l) Positive energy demands discipline and commitment which I lack of.

m) I'd like to explore possibilities that I'd get to know what positive energy means and what it does to my wellbeing gradually.

DAY 1

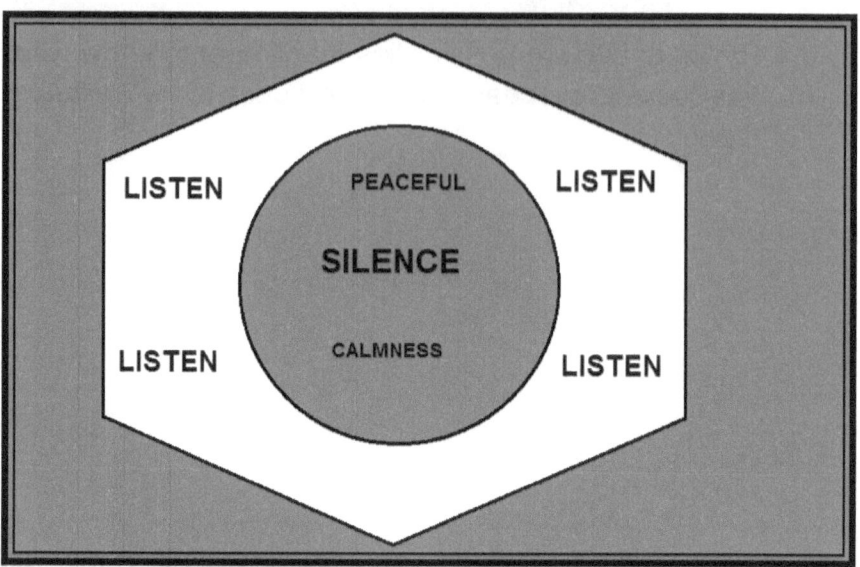

STAGE 3, © Firdevs Dede

Listen to the peaceful silence of calmness without any worry for anything in your life.

1) **Are you aware of total calmness within your body, mind and spirit now?**

   a) Yes

   b) No

   c) Not sure

2) **How do you identify total calmness in your body, mind and spirit?**

   a) I have never experienced total calmness in any sense.

   b) I am a hopeless worrier. I cannot experience total calmness in my body and mind let alone in my spirit.

   c) I am addicted to my daily worries. I can't survive without worries.

   d) All my life time, I had nothing but plenty of worries which kept me on the edge.

   e) I need destructions to be alive but not boring calmness.

   f) I find it difficult to calm down myself.

   g) I am always interrupted by the destructive speed of daily tragedies on media.

   h) It is too much to bear the burden of my friends and their hopeless negativity which keeps me agitated all the time.

   i) I guess total calmness is like being on holiday without any worry about daily struggle of earning a living.

   j) I can't even feel relaxed on my holiday as there is always something worry about like natural disasters, terrorist attacks and being ripped off by the locals.

k) I have some experience of calmness when I cut off myself from daily worries but that is a rare occasion only.

3) **How prepared are you to increase the capacity of your body, mind and spirit to achieve the total calmness?**

   a) I am willing to learn how to become calm and experience inner silence even within the destructive and noisy environment.

   b) It'll be good to have a few tips on how to calm down myself regularly.

   c) I'm prepared to commit myself to a constructive program which would enable me to stay relaxed without any adrenalin rushing in my body all day long.

DAY 1

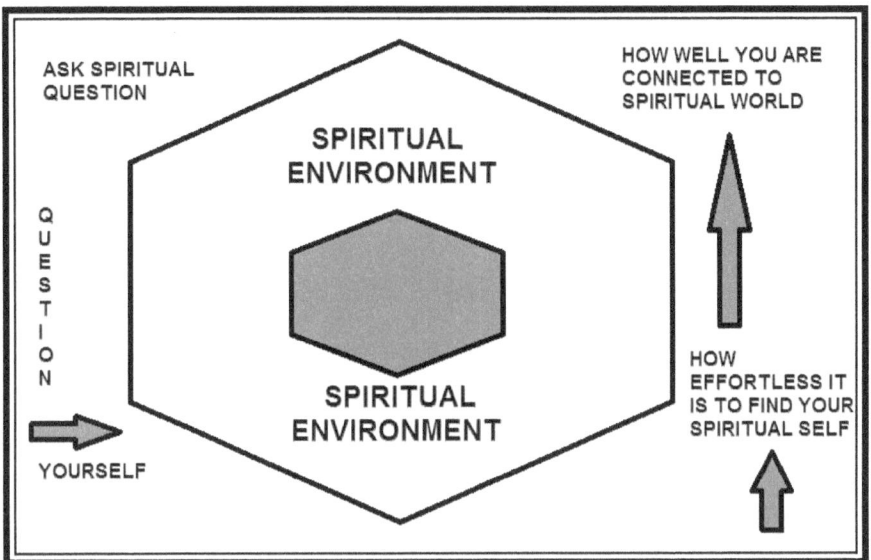

STAGE 4, © Firdevs Dede

Explore how well you are interwoven with the origin of spiritual existence.

1) **Are you aware of your spiritual self now?**

    a) Yes
    b) No
    c) Not sure

2) **Ask yourself what it means to have a spiritual identity?**

    a) I don't have any spiritual existence.
    b) I am completely unaware of my spiritual self.
    c) I feel my understanding of spiritual concepts is limited.
    d) I am completely unease with spirituality.
    e) I am cut off from the spiritual world.
    f) I get on with my daily life which has only materialistic value for me.
    g) I am not sure how it feels to feel your spiritual self. I've never tried before.
    h) I haven't found my spiritual self yet.
    i) I have no intention to get confused with a spiritual identity.
    j) I am better off without any spiritual connection.
    k) It's a waste of time to think about a spiritual identity.
    l) I'd like to find out how it feels to find my spiritual self.
    m) I wish I could be more responsive to my spiritual self.
    n) I'm prepared to commit myself to expand my human capacity to spiritual level.
    o) I'd like to take my spiritual identity to the next level effortlessly.

DAY 1

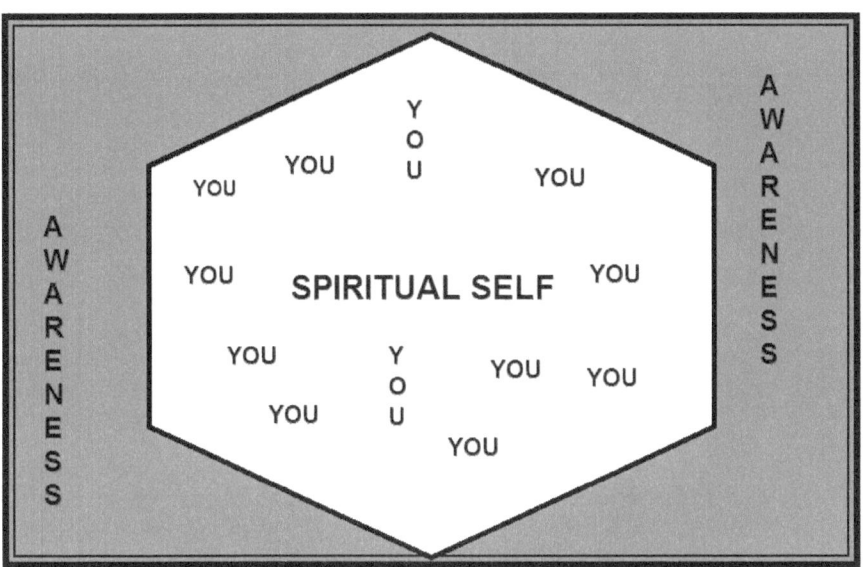

STAGE 5, © **Firdevs Dede**

How to increase your awareness of spiritual identities of others.

Ask yourself what special qualities you usually notice in others.

a) Some people appear to be compassionate and treat everyone with special kindness which makes everyone feel good about themselves.

b) People with spiritual awareness tend to be more conscious about their behaviors by avoiding destructive criticism and conflicts.

c) People with strong spiritual identities also care about others' rights to be themselves.

d) Spiritually mature people are fairer in their daily transactions with others.

e) Some people undermine spiritual identities of others due to a lack of spiritual maturity.

f) People without any spiritual maturity treat others with contempt which causes distress, violence and unhappiness.

g) Spiritual maturity demands a good character with human dignity and calmness.

h) People without any spiritual substance don't care about others' wellbeing as they're after their own advantages.

i) Destructive people usually suffer from a lack of spiritual wisdom.

j) People without spiritual identity always point out the faults of others but not theirs.

k) Absence of spiritual IQ causes a lot of self-destruction in the long run.

l) The bloody battles between good and evil is the outcome of human tragedy which lacks a spiritual wisdom and insight for fairness.

m) Spiritual maturity is only achieved with a positive energy and determination to do good not to ourselves but also others.

DAY 1

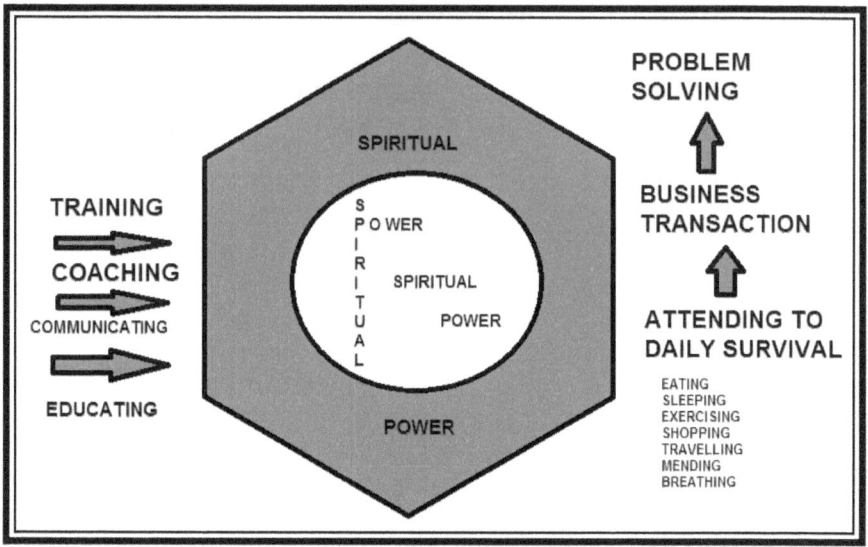

STAGE 6, © Firdevs Dede

How strongly are you connected to spiritual power?

How do you identify your spiritual self in the mornings?

a) I've got good mornings and bad mornings.

b) When it's a good morning, I start my day with a good wish for the whole humanity.

c) When my worries overpower me, I ignore other people's need for my blessings. My ego becomes the center of the universe.

d) I don't feel guilty about focusing on my own wellbeing only. After all, no one really cares about me more than I do.

e) Sometimes, I feel it's my responsibility to care about the whole humanity and think about their wellbeing in my daily spiritual meditation.

f) When I'm fully satisfied with my life, I become generous to include others' wellbeing in my wish list during daily spiritual mediation.

g) Some people don't deserve my spiritual attention, especially, if they ignore my need to be cared for. I can't see the point for including the whole humanity in my spiritual meditation daily.

h) I feel more in tune with my Divine Creator when I start my day with a high profile spiritual meditation which includes all the living beings like animals, plants alongside human beings regardless they are good or bad.

i) I never give up on my spiritual hope that one day there won't be any hatred, unfairness or injustice anywhere in this world. I assume that bad people might change their bad behaviors and decide to become good overnight if I keep on praying for them.

j) Praying for others' wellbeing without getting enough pragmatic outcomes make me feel like giving up praying altogether. Look at the state of the world. There is a plenty of turmoil in politics, economics and daily crimes.

k) I wish a spiritual connection with our Divine Creator could decrease the human agony of being destructive in every aspect of our human lives from education to politics.

l) We live in the most destructive century. Yet, the whole humanity is confused by the different interpretations of the origin of spiritual self.

m) The world religions are turned into a negative division but the believers of each faith lost the spiritual power of uniting the whole humanity for altruistic good causes; the violent acts are taking place all over the world without being stopped by a miraculous revelation of our Divine Creator.

n) No one is sure what is right or wrong anymore which is scary on its own as we can't find common grounds to define basic human values which cannot be changed dramatically from one century to another.

DAY 1

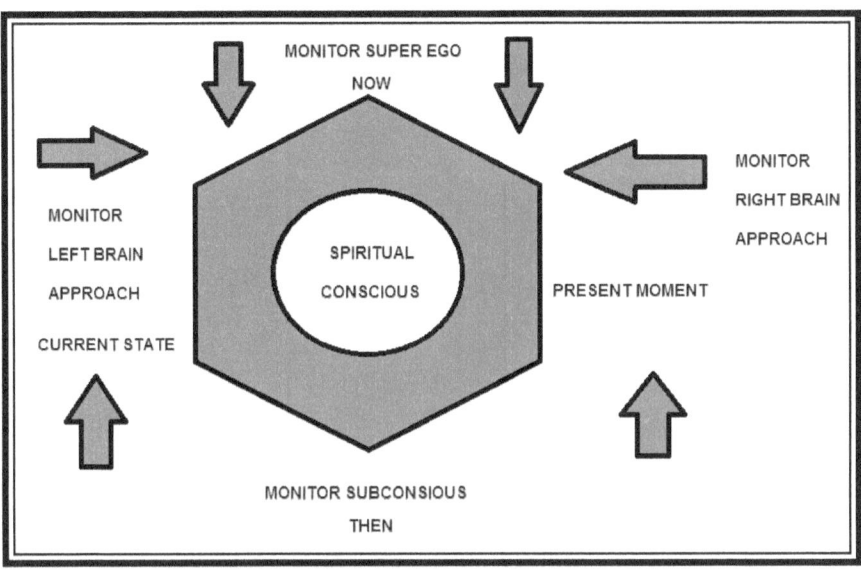

STAGE 7, © Firdevs Dede

How do you monitor your spiritual conscious from moment to moment?

1) **Do you know how to monitor your spiritual conscious?**

    a) Yes

    b) No

    c) Not sure

2) **How intimately do you know your spiritual conscious?**

    a) I've never asked such an awkward question to myself. What for?

    b) I am not sure whether I bear to accept the reality that I've no spiritual conscious at all which is a bit distressing.

    c) It's good to have a spiritual substance of my identity, I suppose. I'm very far away from the hidden potential of my spiritual consciousness now.

    d) I tell the moments of my spiritual conscious when I make important decisions daily such as whether or not to leave a few coins to a waiter.

    e) When I feel too tightfisted, I feel my spiritual conscious isn't working in full capacity.

    f) I always feel thankful to my Divine Creator that I'm still alive after facing a life-threatening disease which made me more aware of my spiritual consciousness.

    g) Once my pet passed away, I become more aware of my spiritual conscious as I've been bereaving for my pet since its dead.

    h) I've started recognizing my spiritual conscious once my daughter lost the battle against cancer. I'm wearing her ashes on my ring as if she is always with me in spirit.

    i) I visit my parents' graves once a year which makes me feel good about myself through spiritual connection.

j) When I spend a quality of time with the people who have got similar awareness of spiritual awareness, it feels spiritually healing.

k) Each evening I go to sleep, I remember of my mortality and remind myself that it might be the final evening of my life which enables me to keep in touch with my spiritual conscious.

DAY 1

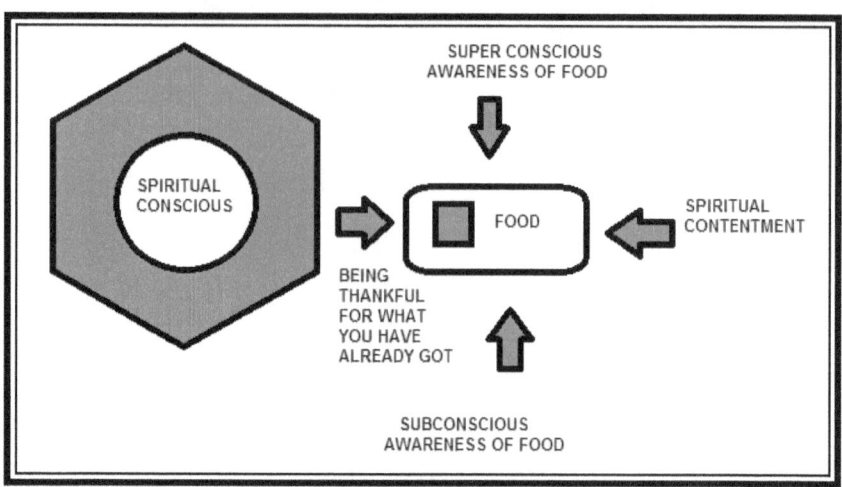

STAGE 8, © Firdevs Dede

How satisfied are you with what you have got?

How often do you examine each fruit, vegetable or any nourishing food you are about to put into your mouth and be grateful to what you have rather than what is lacking in your life?

1) **Do you know how to appreciate what you have got at the moment?**

   a) Yes
   b) No
   c) Not sure

2) **Ask yourself what makes you content with daily.**

   a) I don't see any connection between what I eat and spiritual consciousness.
   b) The food comes from the supermarket. I can't visualize its origin from seed to plate in a spiritual context.
   c) I am not fully aware of what I have got in my life right now in a spiritual sense.
   d) I feel I ought to be content with my earning capacity which is not enough to buy me organic foods.
   e) I am not satisfied with what I have got when I see all the films about the rich people and what they eat.
   f) I think about the starving people each time I am blessed with delicious meals. I pray that all the living beings will have some uncontaminated food and water for their survival as well.
   g) I am more than happy with what I have got without losing the variety of daily food intake. I can't bear the food rationing during the war time.
   h) I thank God for each meal provided for me.

DAY 1

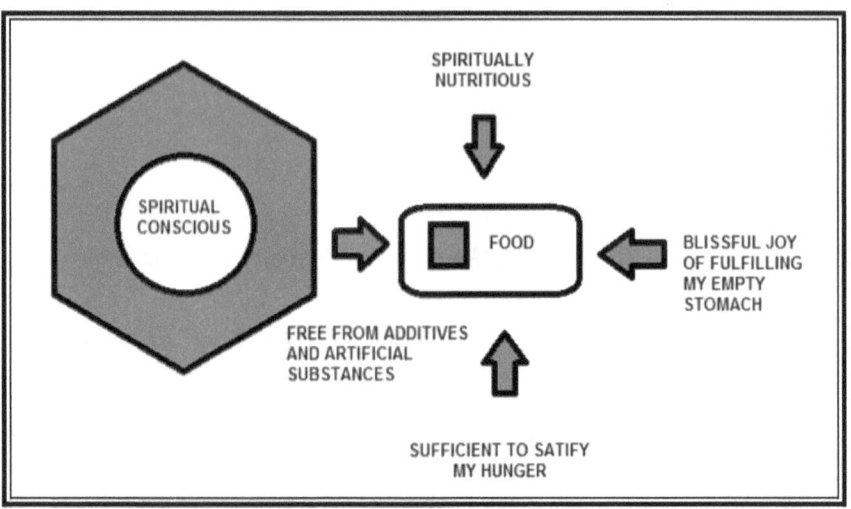

STAGE 9, © Firdevs Dede

Spiritual consciousness for food intake

How accurately do you describe each food you take in?

1) **Are you fully aware of what you eat?**

   a) Yes

   b) No

   c) Not sure

2) **How competent are you to differentiate your senses for each food intake from having raw fruits to simple and complex meals daily?**

   a) I cannot recognize taste, texture or aroma of each fruit as accurately as I might describe vegetables. I don't like fruits.

   b) I am not sure about how to describe what I eat. I enjoy eating but I don't like intellectualizing the eating process.

   c) Sometimes, I am focused on what I eat and satisfied by its taste physically rather than its nutrition or spiritual experience of eating.

   d) I examine fruits and vegetables for their texture, color, taste, aroma and I feel so privileged that I experience each food in a holistic way with multisensory spiritual awareness.

   e) I would certainly like to explore food intake under the light of spiritual consciousness which is completely new concept for me.

DAY 1

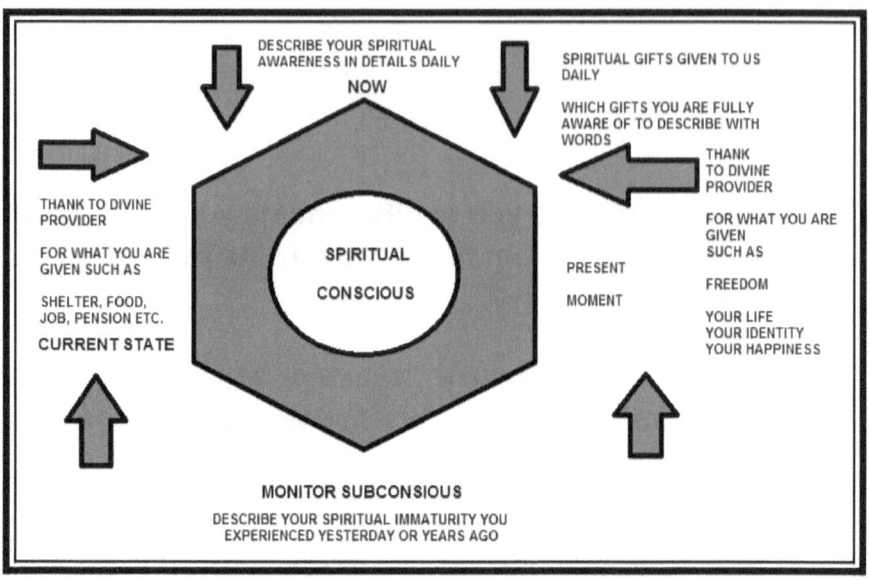

STAGE 10, © Firdevs Dede

How thankful are you for the gifts you possess?

How often do you feel thankful to our Divine Provider for the gifts you were given such as your life; the basic and essential ingredients of your human existence such as food, shelter, freedom & other privileges you possess?

1) **Do you feel thankful for God's gifts you've received so far?**

   a) Yes

   b) No

   c) Not sure

2) **Ask yourself when was the last time you felt grateful to our Divine Creator for the things you were given?**

   a) I cannot really remember when the last time was I felt fully content and thanked to God for that.

   b) It was the time my first son was born. I felt that he was given to me by my Divine Creator like how my own life was given to me, perhaps.

   c) Most of the time, I take everything for granted without giving too much thought about the gifts of God. I think I don't appreciate what I've got wholeheartedly.

   d) When I faced mortality of my loved ones few years ago, I realized that how fortunate I had been to have connections to those important people before they all passed away. After a while, daily worries took over as usual and never thought about the precious gifts of any kind until now.

   e) I became more aware of how precious my health was after losing my health for a while.

   f) Regaining my health made me feel that I should be grateful to God every single minute.

   g) I am a person who lacks the sense of valuing what I've got in my life.

h) There is no value attached to my life. I wish I could see my life in the context of spiritual wisdom. Somehow, I can't.

i) I feel I'd like to explore how it feels to appreciate the gift of life and the purpose of being here.

DAY 1

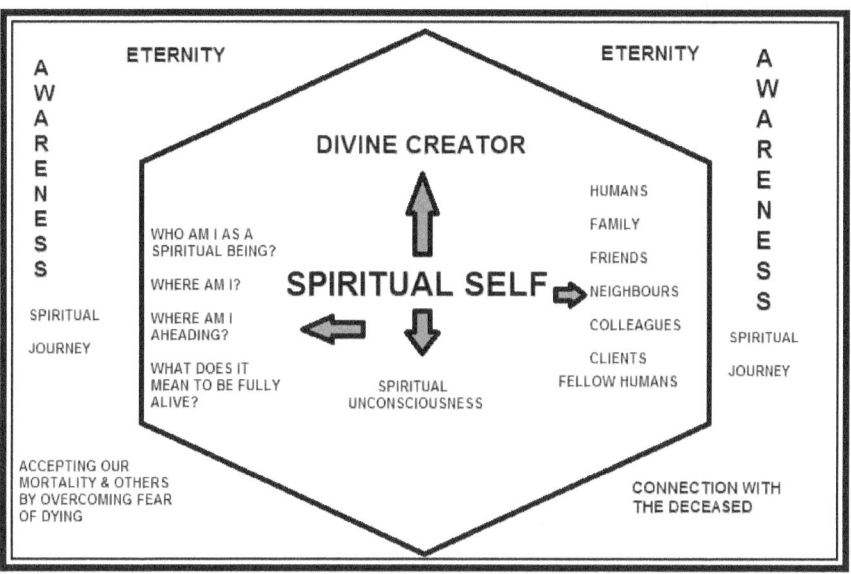

STAGE 11, © Firdevs Dede

The hypothetical questions

Just expand the possibilities with the hypothetical questions of how much you are willing to expand your spiritual awareness of a fulfilling life in spirit & truth.

Some of the hypothetical questions of how far you are prepared to expand your spiritual awareness for a rewarding life in spirit & truth could be listed as follows:

1) **How would you feel if you had a spiritual relationship with your friends, neighbors, employers, employees, children, parents and stakeholders of your community?**

    a) I have no idea how I felt if I had a spiritual relationship with my friends.

    b) I am not sure how others respond to my spiritual need to be connected to them spiritually rather than materialistically at work, education, training and home.

    c) I feel rather apprehensive to think about building up a spiritual connection with others.

    d) I don't think, it's entirely up to me.

    e) The people I am in contact with are all at different stages of their spiritual identity. Some of them don't even have a spiritual IQ as they label themselves atheist.

2) **What does it mean for you to have a spiritual relationship with others?**

    a) I'd like everyone respecting each other as God's Creation rather than their numerical net value. Respecting people for their financial success to have 6 figure earning capacity doesn't make sense to me.

    b) Concept of success needs to be reassessed. What is considered 'Success' for some might be considered 'Failure' for the people with spiritual priorities.

    c) In my view, public recognition for materialistic values such as fame, money, status and political power has no spiritual value.

d) In a spiritual relationship, everyone is treated fairly and equally. No one is inferior or superior. Everyone has got their own unique qualities.

e) A spiritually fulfilling relationship means everyone is welcome to make their decision about how to live with the free will of their spiritual consciousness.

f) No one has got a right to impose their political ideologies on others within a non-imposing spiritual relationship.

g) Sharing spiritual awareness means to commit ourselves to good causes without taking destructive actions e.g. aggressive selling technique is not suitable for people who are spiritually matured.

3) **What is the ideal spiritual transaction with others on a daily basis?**

a) A genuine transparency in our actions without any witch-hunting attitude behind others as consumers, providers, employers, employees, educators, students and fellow human beings.

b) A mutually accepted caring, responsive and beneficial situation without any hidden agenda e.g. no agreement should be signed without breaching consumers' statuary rights for a 2-week cooling period. Any consumer should be able to change their minds if they wish to return the product or services they agreed to purchase in any business premises.

c) Ability to receive and give constructive feedback with the intention of highlighting strengths as well as weaknesses without causing any offence.

d) Without being fooled or tricked by dishonesty.

e) Treating everyone as you want to be treated in any business transaction without hurting, ripping off, taking advantage of, fooling anyone with false allegations or mockery.

f) Respecting everyone's right to be treated with dignity and kindness.

g) Without causing anyone bodily harm and verbal abuse physically or using electronic devices, microchips with high tech equipment like it is practiced by criminal gangs for Electronic Stalking and Mind Control (ESMC) torturing method, which should be banned by the authorities.

DAY 1

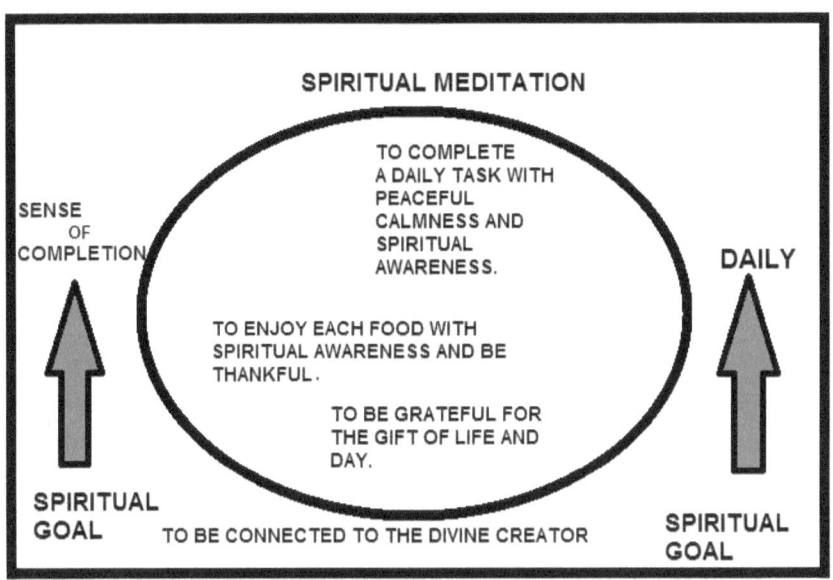

STAGE 12, © Firdevs Dede

Daily spiritual goals

List the most important spiritual goals you aim to achieve throughout your day, today.

Think about what matters to you just now which increase your spiritual fulfilment.

Plan your day with a specific spiritual goal which makes you feel connected to your spiritual self. The followings are some examples, I've come up with.

1) Remembering to water a plant with the awareness of the nourishing water and its impact on a plant to survive is a spiritual experience.

2) Replying to an email with the same pleasant gesture of emotive symbol e.g. smiling face from the respondent just to reassure him/her wellbeing that their effort of being considerate makes me connected to them.

3) Answering a phone call with a warm and pleasant manner which makes the caller feel good about their effort to reach me is spiritually fulfilling.

4) Giving useful information to a person without making any profit for it apart from gaining a spiritual satisfaction teaches me the value of selfless act.

5) Making referral on to other providers without taking a commission for that makes me feel spiritually satisfied for my super spiritual ego.

6) Giving up a seat for a disabled passenger on a public transport willingly without any bad feelings of standing up during the long journey has got a spiritual bonus for my spiritual wellbeing.

7) Sacrificing from my weekly food shopping in order to buy a present for an elderly person while I am experiencing a shortage of weekly income makes me feel good about myself spiritually. Each giving away in hardship has got more value than giving away in abundance.

8) Giving a constructive book review to an unknown author without charging for the review is good for my spiritual development.

9) Helping someone to stand on their own feet after seeing them experiencing a bad fall increases my self-respect at a spiritual level.

10) Buying a sandwich and a bottle of water for a tramp by reducing my weekly shopping makes me feel better than ignoring their suffering.

11) Attending a private view of a less-known artist with a book dedicated to their wellbeing makes me fulfilled by recognizing their achievement.

12) If someone misinterprets my selfless generosity, I usually ignore their misbehavior just to give them a chance to correct themselves.

13) Keep on being selfless by ignoring the fact that unselfish acts are misinterpreted by spiritually immature people.

DAY 1

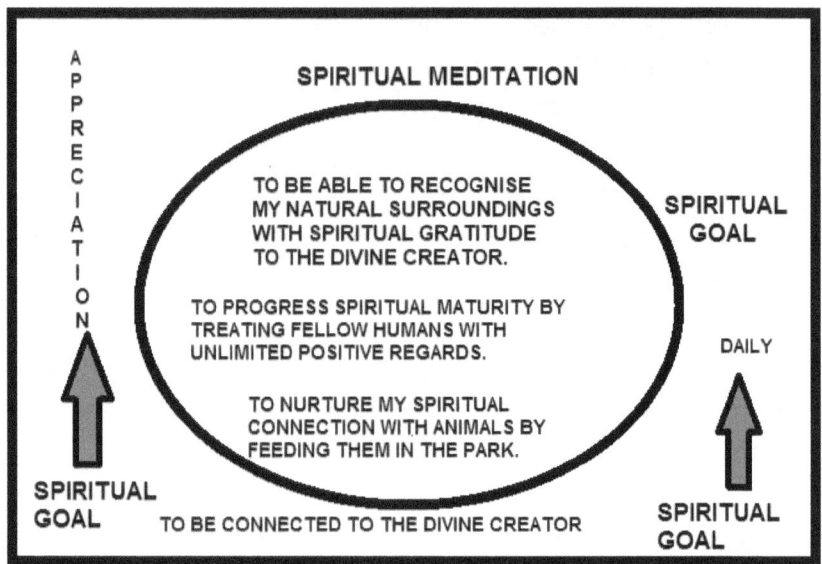

STAGE 13, © Firdevs Dede

The dimension of spiritual goals for inclusiveness

Ask yourself whether or not your spiritual daily goal includes other living beings such as animals and vegetations like plants, flowers and trees apart from human beings.

Ask yourself how to expand your spiritual goals to other living beings such as ecological systems within the vast scale of our cosmos.

1) Feeding squirrels in the park is as fulfilling as feeding starving human beings at a spiritual level.

2) Pondering around the positive ideas about how our inputs could change the future of humanity, animals and ecological systems of our planet has got a spiritual meaning.

3) Working on the positive energy and discarding the negativity from our human approach to daily circumstances is proven to be a constructive step for our spiritual growth.

4) Expanding our micro environment to macro scale could increase our connection to the entire cosmos through a spiritual transformation from a microscopic existence to infinite and ageless beings.

5) A thought process should gain a spiritual dimension with values of our own when we face the scarcity of caring, meaningful and spiritually fulfilling relationship on any business interaction.

6) A genuine spiritual system could overcome a lack of belief system by replacing a fear of being oppressed with an acceptance of all the individuals without any political biases of human destruction within a historical context.

7) The way forward approach in spiritual breakthrough is to accept the limitations of divisive practices within hierarchical top down or vertical business relationships without respecting one another's spiritual identity.

DAY 1

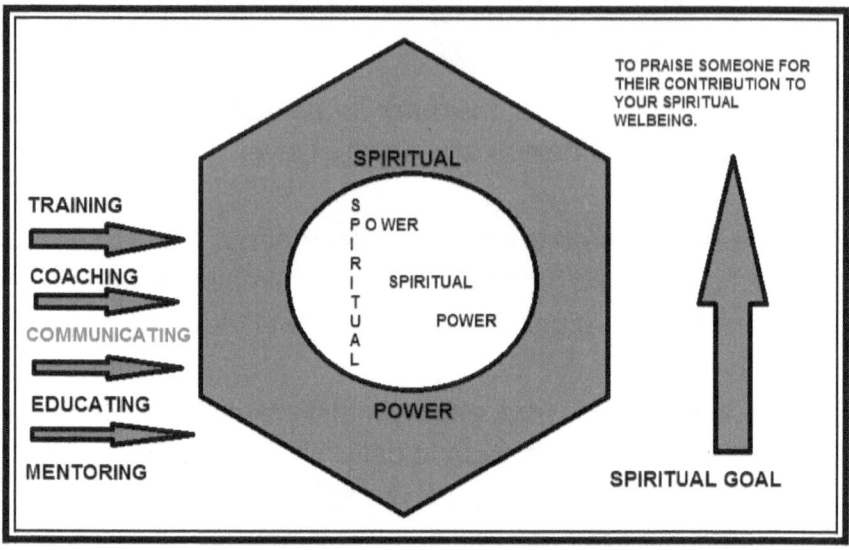

STAGE 14, © Firdevs Dede

Readiness to share spiritual awareness with others

How strongly are you prepared to share your spiritual awareness with others today?

How are you going to share your spiritual awareness with others today?

1) Talking about flowers inside the room and praising their beauty sincerely without worrying about making fool of myself as a meaningful ice breaker.

2) Offering a spiritual insight to others such as how I value the current moment of being with them in a peaceful gesture without worrying about possible misinterpretation is a spiritual breakthrough.

3) Showing my appreciation of others with clear and positive words is a good spiritual practice.

4) Recognizing the power of Divine coincidences for making new connections with spiritually matured individuals who could make positive impact on my wellbeing.

5) Telling our colleagues clearly how important it is to meet and work together in peace while hatred and human destructions is on the rise in the world.

6) Asking others how they find meeting me in terms of spiritual connection.

7) Giving my business card just to make a spiritual connection but not necessarily a business transaction allows me to go beyond materialistic boundary.

8) Wishing others best with their commitments makes me recognize their contribution to group development.

9) Thinking about the positive points first while I am asked to fill in the feedback form.

10) Sending a follow-up email to the new contacts and letting them know how much I valued the time I spent with them personally is good for my spiritual-wellbeing.

DAY 1

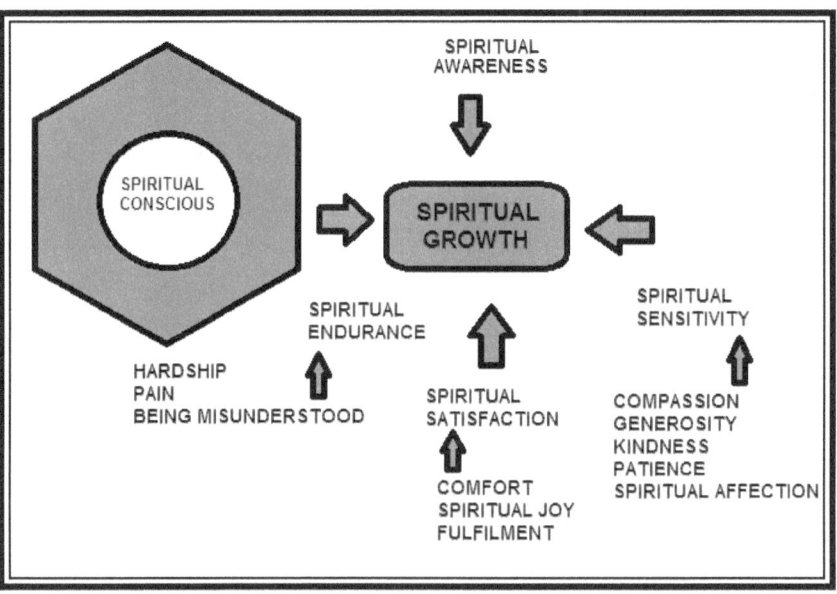

STAGE 15, © Firdevs Dede

Recording spiritual accomplishments

What happens if you consciously record each spiritual accomplishment regularly?

Please record each spiritual accomplishment you achieve daily or weekly on a regular basis.

1) Keeping a spiritual diary will increase awareness of our spiritual maturity.

2) Recognizing what hurts others as well as ourselves could be a starting point for becoming spiritually more sensitive to our concerns and others.

3) Remembering details of sensitive actions by identifying them in writing will help us to increase our spiritual perceptions in the long run.

4) It is possible for us to monitor how perceptive we become to awareness of our inner self when we read our recordings of spiritual growth say in a year time or a decade.

DAY 1

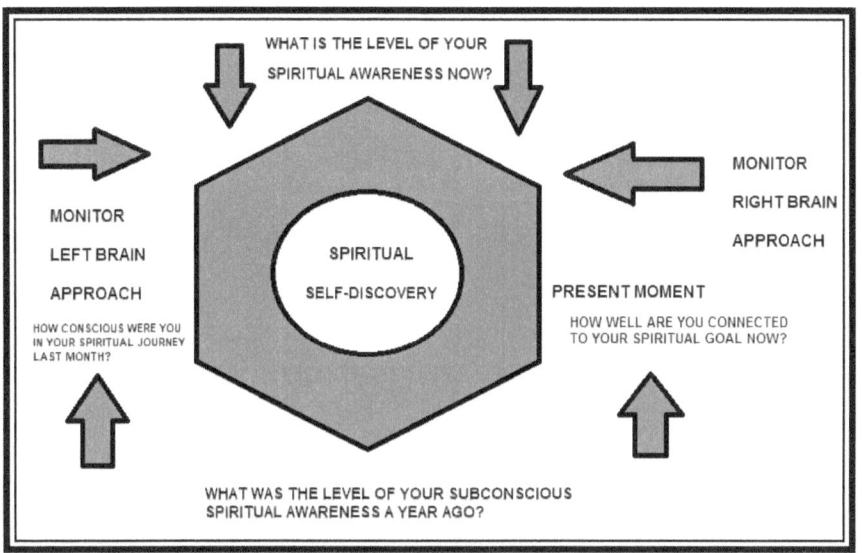

STAGE 16, © Firdevs Dede

Differentiation of spiritual awareness

Just pay attention to how you respond to each spiritual growth process while you are recording your spiritual accomplishments which differentiate your own self-discovery from yesterday, last week, a month ago or a year ago.

Ask yourself where you were a year ago, a month ago, last week and yesterday in terms of your self-discovery in your spiritual journey.

1) **In my spiritual journey, the followings were recorded as my self-discovery a year ago.**

    a) I wanted to use my photography expeditions as a spiritual self-discovery.

    b) The places I visited had been recorded such as landscapes and seascapes through my photographic work.

    c) I recorded the hardship I endured in my audio diary. I identified what type of troubles I have been experiencing.

    d) I looked for spiritual answers when I watched human destructions in conflicts.

    e) I decided to write a book based on my first-hand experience of observing human destructions taking place on a global scale.

2) **What spiritual development I achieved a month ago.**

    a) I decided to take a voyage for a week to take my mind off from the external destructions.

    b) I asked myself questions what I would like to do next amongst the unsettled world of political conflicts.

3) **What spiritual development I recorded since last week.**

    I have disciplined myself to think about my spiritual growth every single day while I was writing this book on a daily basis.

DAY 1

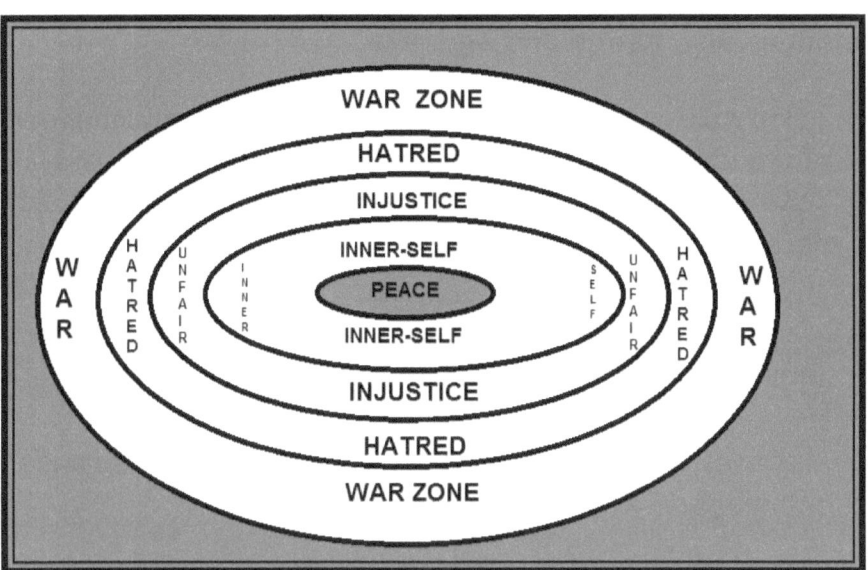

STAGE 17, © Firdevs Dede

Finding inner peace through spiritual wisdom

How often do you look at your inner self with peace without any influences of destructive external interferences such as war, hatred or injustice?

Jot down what you focus on your inner self with peace without any influences of destructive external interferences such as war, hatred and injustice.

1) Stop watching news for a while in order to detox my inner-self from hatred, destructive nature of violent people, useless civil wars, political conflicts, natural disasters, famine and economic problems.

2) I spare some time during the day to mediate with positive energy.

3) I travel for uninterrupted long walks by the seaside/countryside where it is possible to be alone.

DAY 1

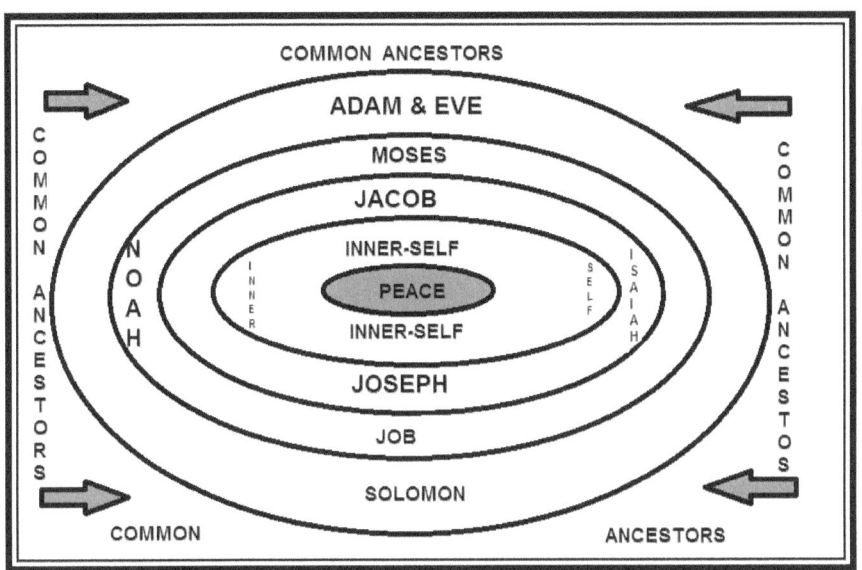

STAGE 18, © Firdevs Dede

Connecting to our common ancestors via a spiritual tree

What happens when you are connected to the great spirits of our common ancestors?

Jot down your spiritual awareness of the Spiritual Tree going back to the first ancestors.

1) I take a great comfort from seeing the big picture without any division of political or religious beliefs of humankind.

2) I feel more compassionate towards the whole humanity when I place myself within the Spiritual Tree of Our Human Ancestors.

3) I become more optimist for a better future for the whole humanity when I am mediating regularly.

4) I realize I am more in tune with our common ancestors Adam and Eve than their off-springs with the useless hatred they demonstrate for one another in the forms of civil wars, cold wars and trade wars.

DAY 1

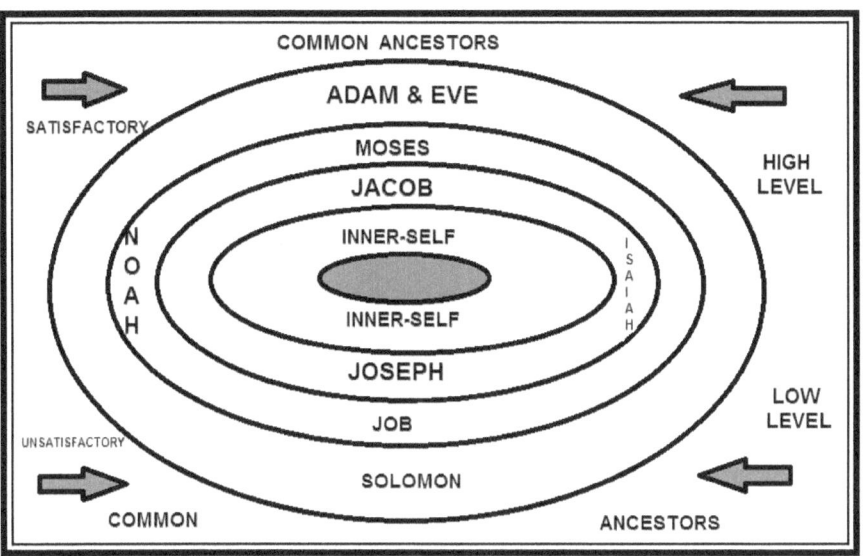

STAGE 19, © Firdevs Dede

Invisible connections through meditations

How well are you able to describe the invisible connection with the great spirits of our common ancestors?

Ask yourself whether you experienced any spiritual connection with our common ancestors at any time in your life.

1) Yes
2) No
3) Not sure

If your answer is yes; please define how you felt and jot them down as you are re-exploring your spiritual identity now.

a) It is a privilege for me to relate to our first ancestors Adam and Eve as I am able to sense their characteristics within our human nature.

b) It feels like Adam and Eve are still amongst us as we're all their off springs.

c) Seven billion children of Adam and Eve possess the genes of our common ancestors; funnily enough, I am one of them.

d) It is good to visualize that Adam and Eve discovered this world in the same way we've been discovering; yet, they didn't have any human parents.

e) I often think about the dilemma Adam and Eve experienced without having any human ancestors before they were created.

f) It might have been a good feeling for Adam and Eve to multiply and observe how their genes passed on to their children by miraculous events.

g) How sad it is to realize that many people are deprived from a spiritual connection to our mutual ancestors.

h) All the negativity human beings experience on this earth is the outcome of disconnection with our mutual ancestors such as Adam and Eve.

i) If everyone is able to reconnect to their origins, there won't be any war among the different races, tribes or generations as we all belong to the same big world family.

DAY 1

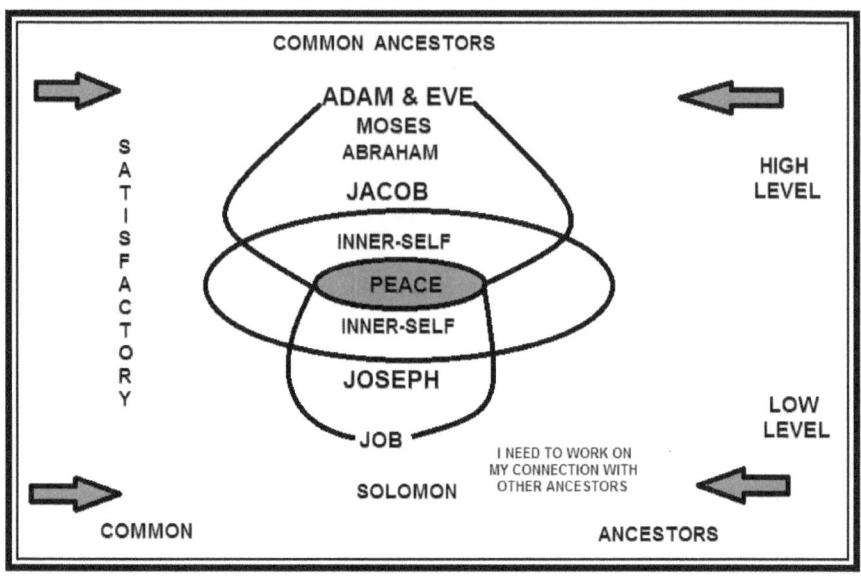

STAGE 20, © Firdevs Dede

**Locate your spiritual connection
with our common ancestors**

Where are you now in terms of your connection with the great spirits of our common ancestors?

Please describe to whom you feel spiritually connected amongst our common ancestors now.

a) I think Job's life story resonates with my life story each time I lose my earning capacity.

b) I always feel that I will be rewarded if I don't lose my hope in the same way Job did when he lost everything including his wealth, health and children.

c) One day, I will be regaining my full earning capacity like Job did when he was confronted with all forms of misfortune.

d) I don't put my hope in lottery but I put my hope in God's grace and kindness.

e) There is always a reward once the trial of being a human being is completed with endurance and patience.

f) Job believed in God's mercy and refused to give up on hope; I do the same.

g) I feel Job lived in the similar way I have been living by getting on with misfortunes when things go wrong in my life circumstances.

DAY 1

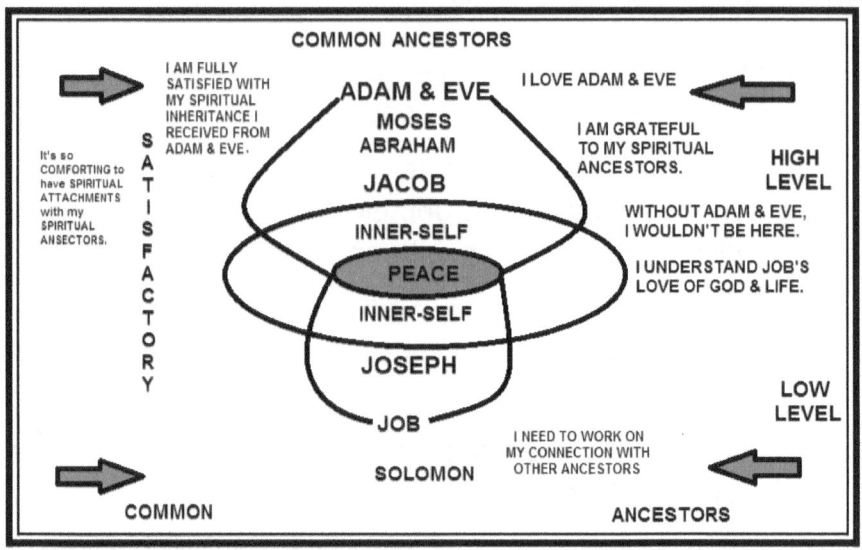

STAGE 21, © Firdevs Dede

Identify the depth of your spiritual connections

How deep is your connection with our common spiritual ancestors?

Just describe the mood you are experiencing with a few expressions that others may understand how you feel now.

1) I feel that God is with me all the time and the sense of belonging to God comforts me.

2) I understand how Job felt when he faced his misfortunes one after another.

3) It is a warm feeling to be reassured by God that my needs will always be taken care of.

4) I am in peace with God's Compassion for His Creations.

5) I know that there is nothing hard for God to do. Our lives depend on God's grace and miraculous coincidences.

DAY 1

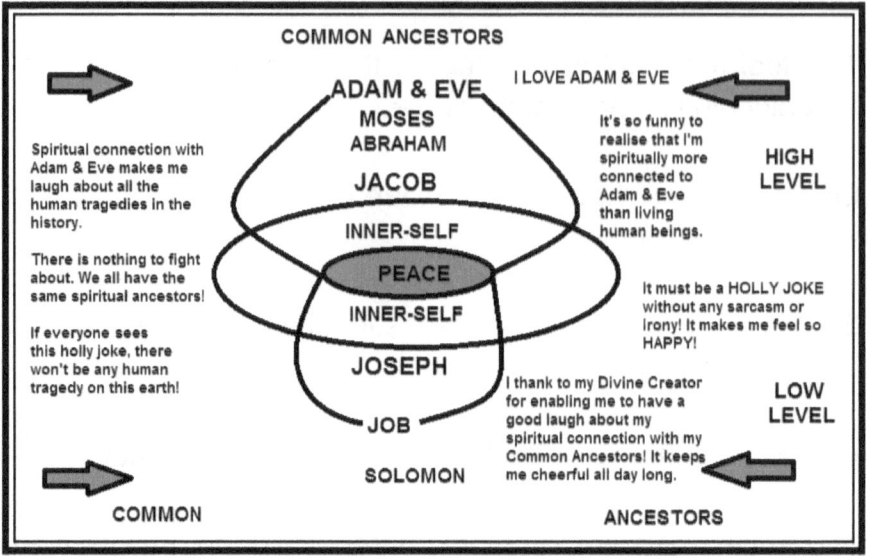

STAGE 22, © Firdevs Dede

Spiritual joke and spiritual joy

a) Does it feel like a joke to have spiritual connection to our common ancestors?

b) How funny is the joke of a connection with our common ancestors amongst the human tragedy?

c) Can you describe how it feels to be in a mood of a spiritually joyful nature?

DAY 1

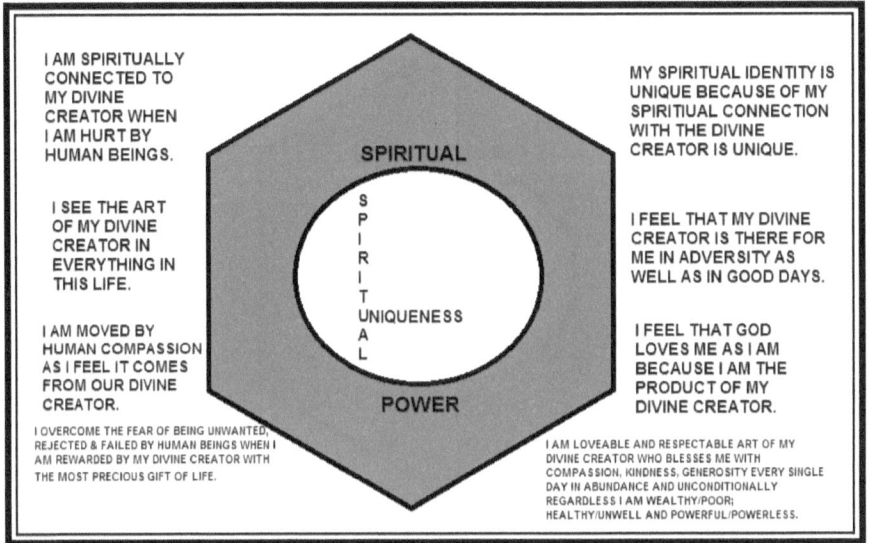

STAGE 23, © Firdevs Dede

Uniqueness of your spiritual awareness

a) What makes your spiritual awareness unique from others?

b) Please write about it and remember it each time you are asked to define your spiritual uniqueness which differs from others.

DAY 1

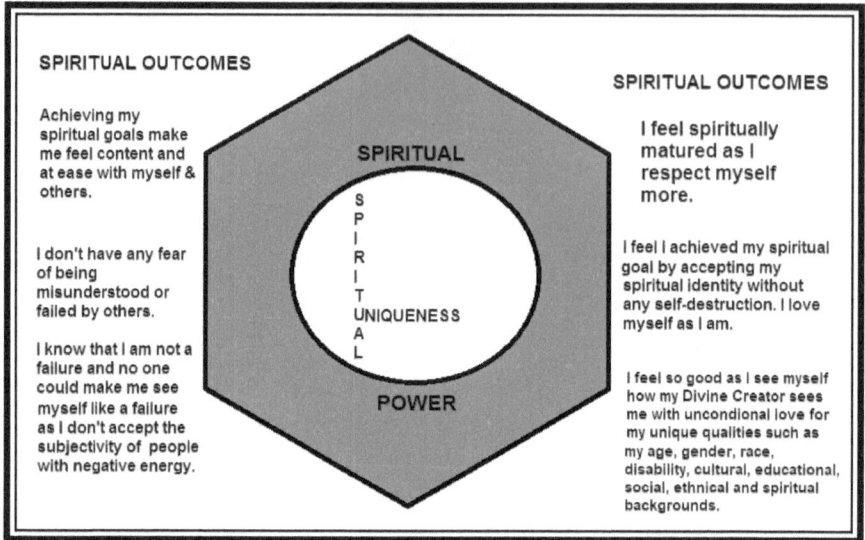

STAGE 24, © Firdevs Dede

Monitor your current state of spiritual mood

How are you feeling after doing the lengthy exercise for raising your spiritual awareness?

DAY 1

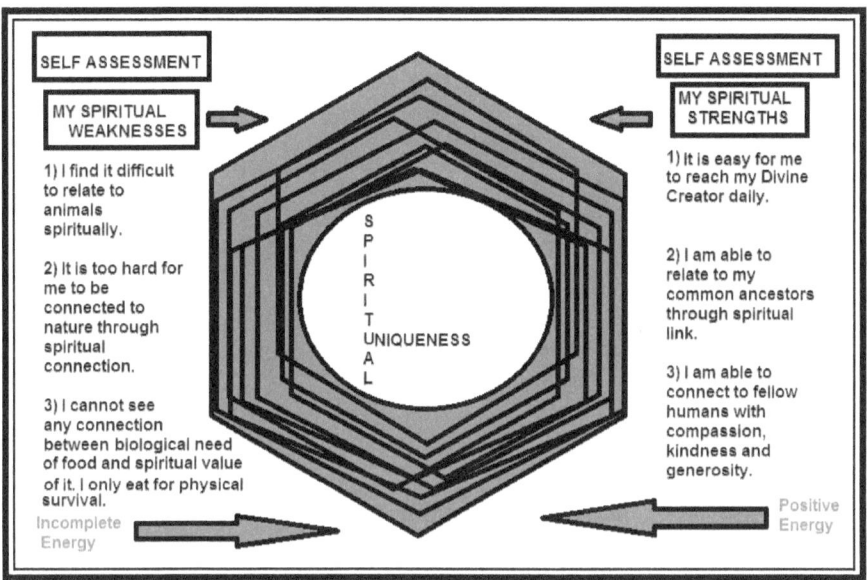

STAGE 25, © Firdevs Dede

Self-assessment of your spiritual growth

Please be honest now and tell yourself how useful it has been to do these exercises. Remember you are your own assessor to assess what works for you and what doesn't work for you. Then, ask yourself how you may improve your **SPIRITUAL GROWTH** from where you are and where you would like to be during the next 6 months, a year time or 5 years' time. You've got a moral right to plan your spiritual growth within your unique sense of time.

Day 1

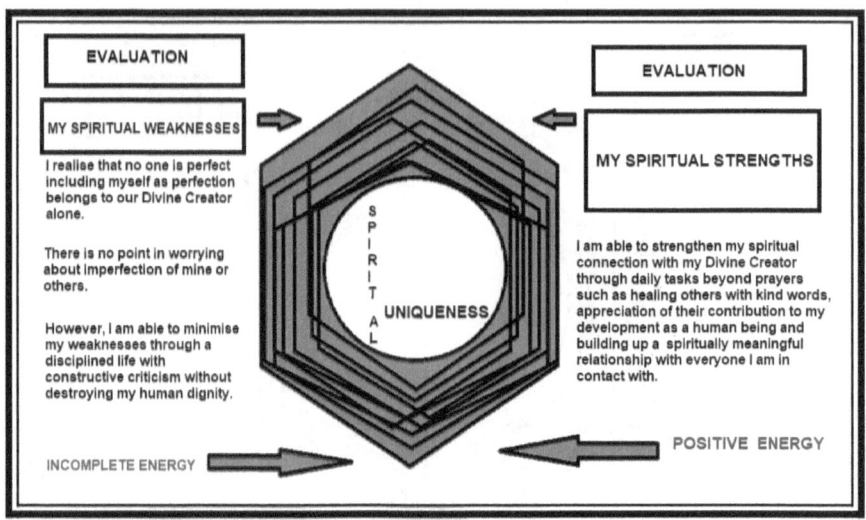

STAGE 26, © Firdevs Dede

Self-evaluation

How will you expand all the exercises you have been experimenting with me further? Please jot down all your thoughts and check them out against your achievements as you go along. Then, praise yourself without underestimating your own effort. Say, well done to yourself when you achieve a great deal even within the milestone of your capability. Ask yourself what else you are able to achieve if you are rewarded with another day, another month or another year on this earth. Then, share your achievements with others. You should be able to reveal your achievements to others generously without worrying about the possibility of being misunderstood such as showing off. Never mind the risk of being underestimated as a spiritually matured person beyond the pragmatic experiences of materialistic approaches to earthy existence! Don't forget if you don't demonstrate what you are capable of achieving in your own life, some people with negative energy will easily undermine your abilities, skills, endurance, life-long achievements and fail you for life which you cannot afford to accept as your spiritual fulfilment will be diminished by negativity even at a subconscious level and you will start seeing yourself inadequate by adopting the lens of your destructive critiques. Then, you will reach the same point where you have started before fulfilling your spiritual goals. Please do not give a second chance to your destructive critics with negative energy to destroy the good work you have already accomplished all the way working through your weaknesses and strengths without giving up when you were confronted by their damaging feedback or conspiracies against you. This world could be a better place if your competitors learnt that they had a chance to better themselves if only they gave up their negativity and worked on their spiritual goals to become better human beings with spiritual values alongside their professional goals. Any goal deprived from spiritual value, does not serve its purpose in life. Any business transaction without genuine compassion, kindness, appreciation of others and unconditional trust is bound to cause a disaster effect which will hurt all the people involved with. Just think about a marriage bond between the partners and what happens once they start cheating each other. Alternatively, think about the faulty product you bought with a high price, how would you feel if you couldn't get a refund for it. Think about the false allegation/s you might have faced in your life. How did you feel when your life was ruined by the negative people's deceit? You could have an endless list of the wrong treatments of the destructive people you have met so far. Reflecting on the damages the destructive people caused to your personal and professional life is a good reminder of not repeating the same patterns of being fooled again. However, it'll be more constructive if you leave all the negative experiences aside now and start thinking positive, doing positive and living your life with spiritual fulfilment without allowing negative people's damaging comments to ruin your human dignity in any way. Please don't forget that the sooner you become the master of your own destiny, the better fulfilment you will accomplish in your spiritual life which leads you towards happier and healthier maturity. Thus, you will be an accredited Wellbeing Coach of Yourself with the mastery of the spiritual goals you have fulfilled while you were doing spiritual exercises designed here for you to explore further at your spare time! I enjoyed writing this book while I was visualizing my fellow human beings who have been experiencing some kinds of misfortune in their lives including our common ancestors. I realize how easy to ignore others' sufferings when we are experiencing our own misfortunes within the hostile environment of this century by being exposed to so many human destructions day in and day out. Writing this book gave me a special purpose which strengthen my confidence in the goodness of humanity for a better future. I hope that **The Business Wellbeing Coach, Unity of Hexagons** will provide an alternative reward for the readers who are willing to endure the pain of doing spiritual exercises by confronting their biases and reaping the harvest of their determination to make a positive impact on others' lives as well as theirs. Let's hope that our common ancestor Job's spirit will stay upon us till the very end, just to remind us his sufferings and rewards he was blessed with by our Creator's Grace alone!

TODAY

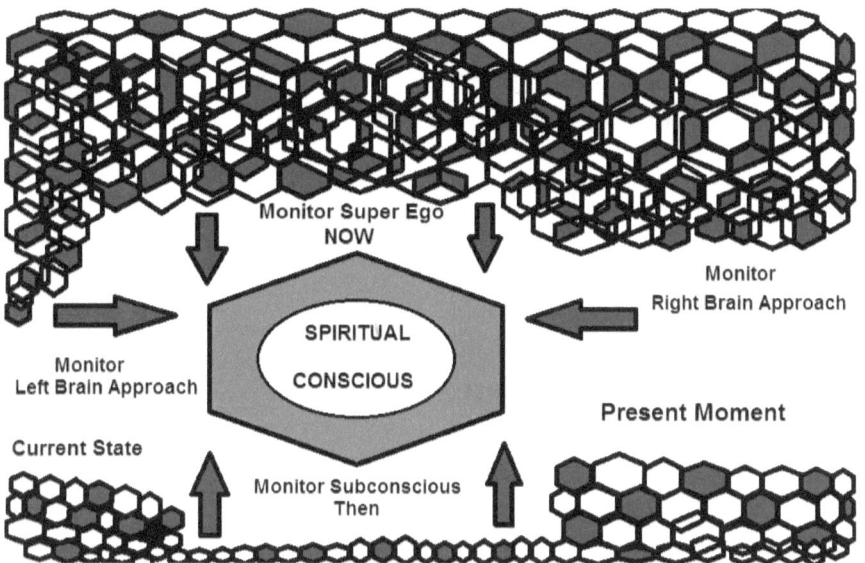

STAGE 27, © Firdevs Dede

Unity of Hexagons

Once we reach our destination with the Unity of Hexagons, life becomes balanced with the combination of body, mind and spirit as there won't be any tragedy of 'Drama Triangle' to suffer from. Instead, we will be capable of experiencing the Unity of Hexagons in the same way honey bees work for their daily patterns of honey combs without losing a track on what they want to create within a harmonious big picture of their bee community. No one is left out distressed, unskilled or unwelcome. Each person is appreciated for their contribution to their community with the similar satisfaction a honey bee might have at the end of a busy day in arts, social science, medicine, education, politics, economics, businesses of small, medium and large sizes in local and global environments as well as in our domestic space with our domestic duties and responsibilities. Consequently, we will be able to record our '**Memoir of Bliss**' at the end of each day instead of worrying about conspiracies, witch-hunts, brutal military coups, terrorist attacks, scam companies and the exploitation of all kinds we might experience at a personal level.

I would like to end my monologue with one of my poems as a gesture to forget yesterday and its agony in order to make the most of today, just now!

Memoir of Bliss

Feel the moment of bliss at present
Never mind the gloomy past
Don't bother with the unpredictable tomorrow
Take the day as it comes
Regret not
But live in the moment of bliss as you please

© Firdevs Dede, 2006

Press Review, 2011

Author debut with a book that explores the life with many faces

New novel focuses on the central character when she fulfills her dream!

LONDON – (Release Date: December 2011) – DREAM Foundation is about Nuala and her distinctive sensitivity at the peak of her creative life as a successful concert pianist. Nuala's genuine love story with her musicologist husband Joshua, who shared Nuala's passion for music provides a good reading. At a mature age, Nuala turns her dream into a reality not only for herself, but for others too. Why don't you discover how Nuala's DREAM Foundation united artists with diverse backgrounds to contribute to the various art forms world-wide such as literature, philosophy, conceptual art, digital art, film making, acting, sculpture, painting and textile? DREAM Foundation is for you all!

About the Author

Firdevs Dede is a British writer. She is a visual artist and a qualified art teacher. Her poetry book, 'The Unfinished Journey' will be appearing shortly with her poetry produced between

1977 and 2011. The poet outlines the essence of her artistic background and how her first novel came about with the comprehensive analysis of her writing style in her academic diary entitled 'Reflections' produced between 2007 and 2011 which hasn't published yet.

Dede is a specialist dyslexia tutor. She lives and works in London. In her forthcoming novel entitled '*Dyslexia isn't an obstacle*,' *she* combines the fiction with the reality of a challenging life style of a dyslexic person by providing a new insight into the complex nature of dyslexia.

DREAM Foundation by Firdevs Dede, 2011

Library of Congress Control Number: 2011907256

Trade Hardcover; **£26.99**; ISBN: 978-1-4628-6942-8

Trade Softcover; **£16.99**; ISBN: 978-1-4628-6941-1

Trade Ebook; **£4.99**; ISBN: 978-1-4628-6943-5

Pages: 499 pages

Book Format: Trade Book 6x9

To purchase copies of the book, please visit **www.XlibrisPublishing.co.uk**. You can also order copies from any bookstore or from me directly **firdevs.dede@gmail.com**.

Dream Foundation by Firdevs Dede, 2011

Genre: Fiction Narrative

DREAM Foundation brings a fresh approach to modern fiction writing with a structure based on short dialogues. How the residences of the DREAM Foundation interact with the legendary pianist Nuala has been depicted with rich symbolism of the modern age. The novel deals with visual art, poetry, science, philosophy and human interactions. It is a good read for readers between 14 and 50+.

Firdevs Dede's View on Philosophy

Philosophy has taken an important part in my personal and literature life. In my book titled: *DREAM Foundation*, I have discussed how I see modern philosophy in relation to art products as follows:

> 'In modern era, philosophy became a thought process and it lost its connection with human emotions. Philosophy has been turned into politics. That's the real struggle in the modern age. Unfortunately, everything including modern art is influenced by the modern philosophy. If we look at any art movement within the modern art history, you can easily find the artwork produced under the strong influence of some materialistic thoughts of philosophy which represents the current fashion. What happened to the modern philosophy in our time is rather tragic.'

'What happens when philosophy becomes part of politics rather than art of living?'

> 'When a particular philosophy loses its influence on the mass products, some artists' work will become out of fashion. No matter how good and original their artwork might be, no one will pay any attention to the unfashionable artists' work as there is no fashionable philosophy supporting their art product.'

©Firdevs Dede (2011), DREAM Foundation, p.413

Peer Review on Amazon, 2015

DREAM Foundation

Before I begin my review, I just want to say something about the author, Firdevs Dede. I recently read another book by her, and was blown away by her writing style, and extensive knowledge. Her surrealist imagery is unlike any writing style that I've ever seen before. Her brilliance is astounding, and I do believe she will make it far in her writing career. I just finished reading DREAM Foundation and was just as impressed as I was after reading the previous novel I read by her. DREAM Foundation is different, however.

This one focuses on having a deep affection for art and human beings. It is about a woman who was about to give up on her dreams, due to difficult circumstances she had to overcome.

Inspiration soon follows, and Nuala realizes just how important your passions are. The relationship between her and Patricia was very enduring, and truly helped Nuala along the way. This is a complex read but definitely a worthwhile one, and I would highly recommend it. I do plan on going back and reading some of Dede's earlier works, and I can't wait to see what she has in store for us next.

Veronica, 2015

Peer Review on Xlibris, 2011

DREAM Foundation

DREAM Foundation is a fantastic book, full of ideas and various forms of artistic concepts I am using it as an excellent resource for tutorial activities.

I read it from cover to cover and I will read it again and again. My students BTEC Level 2 IT at Lambeth College read it as well and they loved the book. We are going to discuss some of the ideas in our next tutorial.

Keep it up and we hope more publication will come out soon. Well done!

Regards,
Dr. Sheren Abdulrahman
Retired Course Tutor (Lambeth College – BTEC Level 2 IT)

Press Review, 2015

FIRDEVS DEDE CLAIMS 'DYSLEXIA ISN'T AN OBSTACLE' IN NEW BOOK

Dyslexia specialist focuses on strengths of dyslexics but not weaknesses

LONDON – The British Dyslexia Association estimates that dyslexia affects around 15% of population to a lesser or greater extent through the way, information is processed, stored and retrieved, with problems of memory, speed of processing, time perception, organisation and sequencing. Firdevs Dede, a specialist dyslexia tutor who has met hundreds of dyslexic students since 2002, claims that dyslexia should not be an obstacle for a fulfilling and rewarding life. In fact, in her new book, "Dyslexia isn't an Obstacle" published by Xlibris, she demonstrates that the cognitive profile of a dyslexic person could be a gift rather than a disability.

"Dyslexia isn't an Obstacle" sheds light on the daily realities of creative dyslexic people, inspiring those who are dyslexic and educating outsiders who are not familiar with dyslexia. This informative volume follows Felix, a dyslexic, who against all odds becomes a successful entrepreneur. There is humor, misfortune and ultimately triumph interwoven into the young man's remarkable life.

"In my book I focus on what makes dyslexic people unique by highlighting their strengths," Dede says, "I also illustrate how some of the linguistic problems could be dealt with, once new habits are developed using a systematic and comprehensive support program that I carefully design for my learners I work with."

"Dyslexia isn't an Obstacle" is an insightful and empowering book that will prove useful not just to dyslexics but those who want to understand this often misunderstood condition better.

"Dyslexia isn't an Obstacle"
By Firdevs Dede
Library of Congress Control Number: 2015900411
Hardcover | 6 x 9in | 384 pages | ISBN 9781503533646; **£18.02**
Softcover | 6 x 9in | 384 pages | ISBN 9781503533653; **£12.01**
E-Book | 384 pages | ISBN 9781503533660; **£7.49**
Available at Amazon and Barnes & Noble
http://www.threedimensiondyslexia.org.uk

About the Author

Firdevs Dede is a specialist dyslexia tutor who lives and works in London. She offers one-on-one support tuition, coaching, mentoring and consultation in education, training, and dyslexia-related specialist knowledge on a face-to-face basis and online. She has 32 years of experience working with talented individuals. Dede is the founder of Three Dimension Dyslexia. She is a visual artist, poet, novelist, short story writer, photographer, study coach and educator.

Genre: Fiction Narrative

Dyslexia isn't an Obstacle by Firdevs Dede, 2015 / Revised Edition, 2017

Dyslexia isn't an OBSTACLE is a futuristic fiction which reveals the undisclosed strategies of success in education and business from the point of Felix. Everyone will enjoy discovering how Felix became the wealthiest entrepreneur with sense of humor, misfortune and fortune attached to his unique destiny.

Peer Review on Amazon, 2015

Dyslexia isn't an Obstacle

Once I started...I couldn't put it down, Dr. Halbeisen (2015)

Firdevs Dede, is a world-renowned author of three books, academic skills coach and tutor helping students on their higher education. Her brand, Three Dimension Dyslexia, equips students with academic writing and reading skills for research purposes. If that's not enough to rock your world, Firdevs has developed an individualized teaching strategy that enables learners to activate the left hemisphere of their brain alongside their intuitive learning style and in this book, she focuses on what makes dyslexic people unique.

In this book, Firdevs highlights their strengths and how some of the linguistic problems could be dealt once the new habits are developed with a systematic and comprehensive support. Well-structured written in a narrative style, this book is a joy to read.

Who should read this book:

- Students wanting to improve their learning skills to excel at their higher studies or thinking a research career.

- Parents wanting to get an increased self-awareness of learning styles to help your child to be the best he/she can be
- Entrepreneurs wanting to take your business to the level by improving those organizational, time management and presentation skills
- In a nutshell, anyone who likes to use the condition Dyslexia to their advantage and follow the footsteps of Albert Einstein and Sir Richard Branson.

Read the book - just one idea may save you lot of sleepless nights.

Wonderful Read by a Great Author, Veronica (2015)

Being an educator, it's important for me to be aware of, and understand, all different types of special needs that a child may be facing. It's important not only to know how to handle a situation, but also to spot when/if a child may have a problem that has possibly gone undiagnosed. Dyslexia Isn't an Obstacle, by Firdevs Dede, is a wonderful read having to do with people suffering with Dyslexia, and how they are able to still lead normal lives, without it being an obstacle in their lives. Dede works with adults who have Dyslexia, and provides a lot of helpful input based on experience. The book focuses on what makes people with Dyslexia so unique by highlighting the strengths that they have. Linguistic problems can be resolved by setting new habits and routines for kids/people to follow as they go about their day-to-day lives. The author believes that learning should be made enjoyable, which is exactly what most educators believe in. There is quite a bit of humor thrown into this one, to ensure that the reader doesn't get bored. I found this to be a fascinating read that is truly going to help me when it comes to my own students. Great job to Dede for writing such a well informative, easy to follow book about Dyslexia. I highly recommend.

A Very Good Read, Sue (2015)

Dyslexia Isn't an Obstacle by Firdevs Dede is not your average book, it's actually an academic book written to empower students with reading, writing, and critical thinking skills as well as a host of other learning and what I would call life skills. It is designed in a fun and interesting narration in a story form. Although the book was written for people with dyslexia, I found it educational. I always thought dyslexic people just wrote their letters backwards and had a hard time reading but this book opened my eyes to some of what dyslexia is and that it is not really an obstacle or a disability, as so many labelled it, but rather a unique understanding of connections in the world we live in.

The book tells the story of Felix, a young man who is dyslexic. He is a very well-developed character (in fact, all the characters are) and the story starts with him at a rough time in his life when he is homeless and in trouble with the law. Felix never finished school, couldn't read or write well, and his future looked bleak. As the story went on this all changed with the proper therapy and learning techniques which the book does touch on.

An entertaining story in the life of a dyslexic, Anonymous Amazon Customer (2015)

This book was an attention keeper. It was written in an engaging narrative style rather than is an instructional format.

I did enjoy the story about Felix and his hard luck made good story. He was shown the milk of human kindness by his barrister Mr. Goodman.

Through the help of tutors Felix was taught to read and utilize his unique learning style.

Even though he spent two years imprisoned for being homeless and staying in a building without permission. The Goodmans and Steve tutored him to sit for his exams. He was able to continue his education at university afterward.

I especially enjoyed where he made a change of major to one more suited for his strengths and did very well in it.

He overcame his self-esteem issues and reached a happy life.

The reflections he made at the end of the different poles of failure versus success were helpful in understanding the dyslexic person.

I would highly recommend this book to anyone wanting a better understanding of dyslexia without reading an academic text.

I would enjoy more work from this author.

Press Review, 2012

The Unfinished Journey

Description

Firdevs's poetry book '**The Unfinished Journey**' consists of 60 poems and 44 illustrations produced between 1977 and 2011. For the poet, life is a short journey, which could be enriched with an artistic experience depicted in the act of poetry writing over the years. Firdevs Dede is a visual artist and a qualified art teacher. Firdevs explores life with genuine affection for art and human beings by using the surrealist imagery writing technique she has invented herself in her first novel titled 'DREAM Foundation'.

The poet outlines the essence of her artistic background and how her first novel came about with a comprehensive analysis of her writing style in her academic diary entitled: 'Reflections' produced between 2007 and 2011 and is not published yet.

Firdevs Dede is a specialist dyslexia tutor. Firdevs lives and works in London. In her forthcoming novel entitled: 'Dyslexia isn't an obstacle' Firdevs combines the fiction with the reality of a challenging life style of a dyslexic person.

Hardcover; **£23.99** ISBN: 978-1-4653-0226-7
Softcover; **£13.99** ISBN13: 978-1-4653-0225-0
Pages: 169
Book Format: Trade Book 6x9

To purchase copies of the book, please visit
www.XlibrisPublishing.co.uk

You can also order copies from any bookstore or from the author directly **firdevs.dede@gmail.com**.

Genre: Modern Poetry

The Unfinished Journey by Firdevs Dede, 2012

Firdevs Dede's poetry book, The Unfinished Journey, consists of 60 modern poems which have been regarded as an alternative approach to the archaic poetry writing technique by modern poetry enthusiasts. The selected 45 fine art images of digital drawings, textile drawings and freehand drawings enriched the lyrical language within visual space that are displayed in a book format rather than a canvas as poet Firdevs Dede believes that artists' books could be appreciated like art forms for their unique appearances and contents but not for their commercial values!

Peer Review, 2012

The Unfinished Journey

Dear Firdevs Dede

I am sorry not to have responded to your message sooner. Life has been quite busy, especially as we had family staying for a time.

However, I did download a copy of your book of poetry and enjoyed looking at it. I particularly admired the artwork, which seemed to complement the poems very well.

I liked the poems written for your father –they seemed very evocative. I have included a sequence which I wrote about my own father in my new book – details of which I will include below. I was also interested to find the account of your visit to St Ives and the studio of Barbara Hepworth. We have been there several times, and I contributed two poems to a book that was published for the centenary of her birth in 2010.

A.L. (2012)

Genre: Non-Fiction

**Business Wellbeing Coach, Unity of Hexagons
by Firdevs Dede, 2018**

Business Wellbeing Coach, Unity of Hexagons offers a consumer-friendly alternative approach to aggressive selling techniques for ethical business interactions with consumers, clients, patients, suppliers, students, politicians, citizens and community members within any unit of the social construction in modern life style without abusing civil and statuary rights of individuals.

Table 1 (Emotional Intelligence Checklist, 2016); Table 2 (MARA in Politics, 2018); Table 3 (MARA in Education, 2018) are designed to equip readers for self-assessment of their emotional intelligence.

There are 38 articles related to business interactions with analysis of high risk and risk-free communication process. Each article could be used as a starting point for readers to reflect on their own experiences with fellow human beings. The 27 spiritual exercises are designed to raise an awareness of spiritual GROWTH model as part of learning wellbeing strategies.

Audience Level: Adult ages 16 – 90

Category of Genre: Wellbeing, Education, Psychology, Coaching, Business, Ethics, Spiritual Development, Emotional IQ, Self-Help

Author

Firdevs Dede is a Business Wellbeing Coach with 37 years of work experience in public and private sectors. The author of Business Wellbeing Coach makes her living as a dyslexia specialist providing services to dyslexic adults from diverse backgrounds on undergraduate and postgraduate degree courses from humanities to social science & medicine.

Firdevs Dede is a visual artist, a photographer, a novelist, a poet and a short-story writer with a track record of regular publications to contribute to the world cultural heritage sharing her first-hand experiences accumulated during her private research studies and research trips to the selected destinations. Firdevs advocates social inclusion, fairness, freedom of expression, freedom of choice and equality in education and at work. Firdevs promotes business ethics with spiritual awareness of our common ancestors' experience such as Job from the Biblical text for his endurance of misfortune which was rewarded by the divine restoration of his well-balanced fortune.

Firdevs Dede's Services, 2018

SPECIALIST WELLBEING COACHING

- Business Wellbeing Coaching
- Learning Styles Coaching
- Academic befriending Coaching
- Motivational Coaching
- Solution focused Coaching
- Life Skills Coaching
- Multiple Intelligence Coaching
- Recreation Coaching for Self-Development
- Well-Balanced dietary coaching for enhancing brain functions such as retention factual information for exam preparation
- Lateral thinking Coaching

SPECIALIST MENTORING

- Getting to know more about meta-cognitive strategies
- Left Brain and Right Brain Approaches
- Memory Enhancement for reflective thinking
- Interpersonal & Intrapersonal Development
- Adjustment to Work placement

- Dealing with conflicts in education, at work in domestic environment
- Risk Assessment
- Understanding Internal Procedures; Organizational Structures
- Getting to know Health & Safety at Work, in Education or Training
- Continuous Professional Development
- Formal Letter Writing for Job Search
- CV Critique
- Business Start-up
- Expanding Business Structure
- Health and Safety Procedure at work and within educational settings

SPECIALIST TUITION

ACADEMIC STUDY SKILLS

- Speed Reading Strategies for Academic Writing
- Developing Valid Argument for Dissertation & Thesis
- Analytical Thinking Skills
- Evaluative Thinking Skills
- High Level of Critical Thinking Skills

ACADEMIC CONVENTION
Grammar; Punctuation; Citation; Bibliography; Reference List

REPORT WRITING SKILLS
Selecting suitable methods for different report writing

PROOFREADING & EDITING STRATEGIES
Self-evaluation
Identifying strengths to decrease weaknesses

SUPERVISION WITH MA THESIS AND DISSERTATIONS

RESEARCH MANAGEMENT PORTFOLIO
Field Research; Desk Research; Quantitative; Qualitative Research

PRESENTATION SKILLS
Power Point Presentation; Case Study Presentation; Public Speech

IT SKILLS

ORGANISATIONAL SKILLS

TIME MANAGEMENT SKILLS

COMMUNICATION SKILLS
Verbal, written and body language

SPELLING PROGRAMME
Specialist Terminology in Science, Humanities and Teaching Training

CONSULTATION
Consultation is provided in the specific areas as follows.

- **Business Wellbeing for Individuals and Organizations**
- **Nature of dyslexia, dyspraxia, dyscalculia, dysgraphia**
- **Nature of ADHD (Attention Deficit Hyperactive Disorder)**
- **Anxiety Disorder related to dyslexia, ADHD**

CONTACT ME

Please contact me directly via the given emails below. I usually answer written enquiries within 24 hrs.

Firdevs Dede

Email: threedimensiondyslexia@outlook.com
Email: firdevs.dede@gmail.com
Tel: +44 (0)2073940192

Firdevs Dede's Profile

AREA OF SPECIALISM

Adult Dyslexia, Diagnosis & Tutoring, Specialist Mentoring, Business Wellbeing Coaching, Creative Writing, Printmaking, Fine Art, Photography, Business Models and Computer Networking

PROFESSIONAL MEMBERSHIP

DSA-QAG, PATOSS, Association for Coaching, ALCS & DACS

PUBLICATIONS

Aug 2018 Spiritual Mindfulness in Colour - Spiritual Exercises

2018 BWC, Unity of Hexagons – Self-help Book

2016 Memories from Turkey – Photography Book

2016 Art of Volcanic Landscape – Photography Book

2016 Artefacts from Goreme – Photography Book

2016 Istanbul – Photography Book

2016 My Poet Brother – Photography Book

2015 Life is Precious – Photography Book

2015 European Trip – Photography Book

2015 Dyslexia isn't an Obstacle – Fiction Narrative

2014 Triple Journey – Photography Book

2013 Reflective Diary – Photography Book

2013 Fragments of Life – Photography Book

2013 From London – Photography Book

2012 The Unfinished Journey – Poetry Book

2011 DREAM Foundation – Fiction Narrative

1988 From an Unknown Artist's Logbook

QUALIFICATIONS

2015 Personal Performance Coaching Diploma

2009 PGCE Assessing Adult Dyslexia, Diagnosis and Support

2005 CPCAB Counselling Certificate

2004 C&G Teaching Certificate Further Education

2002 C&G Computer Networking Diploma

1993 MA Printmaking, Camberwell College of Arts

1987 Research Studies on Paul Klee, ICA

1986 Diploma in Modern Art History, ICA

1980 BA (Hons) in Arts Education, Marmara University

PHOTOGRAPY RESEARCH & GROUP SHOWS

2017 Research Cruise – Barcelona, Palma de Mallorca, Palermo, Rome, Savona & Marseille

2016 Research Trips – Fethiye, Istanbul, Kalkan, Kas, Goreme

2015 Research Trips – Monaco, Nice, Venice, Barcelona, Malta

2014 Research Trips – Dorset, French Riviera, Falmouth

2013 Research Trips – Broadstairs, Bath, British Riviera

2012 The Strand Gallery – London

2012 The Greenwich Gallery – London

2011 Cafe Gallery – London

2011 Swiss Cottage Gallery – London

1993 Whitechapel Gallery – London

1993 Railings Gallery – London

1993 Final Year Degree Show, Camberwell College of Arts

1991 Frontier Exhibition, Chelsea College of Arts

1991 Arts for Offices Gallery – London

1991 London Institute Gallery 1991 Yarrow Gallery – Northants

1990 Intaglio Printmaker Gallery – London

1987 PRIME ART FAIR – London

(PRIME: Psychological Research Industrial Medical Research)

SOLO EXHIBITION

1988 The Long Gallery, Central Library Wood Green – London

References

A Metaphysical Understanding of Numbers, 2009
Philllips, D., A., (2009). The Complete Book of Numerology, Discovering the Inner Self. USA: Hay House. pp.7, 80.

Article 5 – Equality and Non-Discrimination as part of Convention on the Rights of Persons with Disabilities (2006)
https://www.un.org/development/desa/disabilities/convention-on-the-rights-of-persons-with-disabilities/article-5-equality-and-non-discrimination.html [Accessed on 10 Jan 2018]

Black Women History by Prof. Pero Gaglo Dagbovie, The Journal of African American History,
Volume 89, Number 3, summer 2004; http://www.journals.uchicago.edu/doi/abs/10.2307/4134077 [accessed on 29 Dec 2017]

Categories of self-concept, 2013
Blythe, J. (2013) Consumer Behaviour. UK: Sage Publication Ltd. p.90.

CROWN COURT WITNESS OATH & CROWN COURT WITNESS AFFIRMATION
https://www.nidirect.gov.uk/articles/giving-evidence-court [accessed on 25 Apr 2018]

Experiential Marketing, 2006
Lenderman, M. (2006) Experience the Message, How Experiential Marketing is Changing the Brand World. New York: Caroll & Graf Publishers. p.20.

Strategic Management, 2010
Thompson, J. & Martin, F. (2010) Strategic Management & Change. UK: Cengage Learning EMEA. p.51.

The Holy Bible, 1991
Hayford, J.W. (Editor) et al. (1991) Spirit-Filled Life Bible, New King James Version. USA: Thomas Nelson Publishers. pp.82, 106, 107, 115.

The Quran, in English, 2014
Itani a T.(Author). (2014) QUARAN IN ENGLISH. USA: Createspace Independent Publishing Platform/ Amazon Kindle Edition.

Therapeutic use of self: a model of the intentional relationship by Taylor & Melton, 2009
Edited by Duncan, E., A. (2009) Skills for Practice in Occupational Therapy. USA/UK: Elsevier Limited. p.137.

Trust, Distrust, and Epistemic Injustice by Prof. Katherine Hawley, 2015
https://katherinehawleydotorg.files.wordpress.com/2015/02/trust-distrust-and-epistemic-injustice.pdf [accessed on 02 Apr 2018]

Trust and Distrust between Patient and Doctor by Prof. Katherine Hawley, 2015

https://katherinehawleydotorg.files.wordpress.com/2015/02/trust-and-distrust-between-patient-and-doctor-final.pdf [accessed on 02 Apr 2018]

Whistleblowing Guidance for Employers and Code of Practice (2015)

https://www.gov.uk/whistleblowing [accessed on 01 Feb 2018]

Forthcoming Publication, 2019

Firdevs Dede's Poetry & Ethnographical Composition, 2019

Firdevs Dede's two poems titled **The Needle Worker's Dictionary** (2004) and **Void** (2005) were composed by Ethiopian Krar Composer Ras Steven Rogers in 2016. Firdevs Dede aims to publish a complete album based on her poetry with its Ethnographic Compositions to celebrate her 60th birthday for a new chapter in her life during the summer 2019.

www.ingramcontent.com/pod-product-compliance
Lightning Source LLC
Chambersburg PA
CBHW020633220526
45464CB00001B/128